THE JOY OF COMPASSION

MAY THE BUDDHADHARMA REACH ALL SENTIENT BEINGS · LAMA YESHE WISDOM ARCHIVE ·

LAMA ZOPA RINPOCHE

The Joy of Compassion

Edited by Nicholas Ribush

LAMA YESHE WISDOM ARCHIVE • BOSTON

www.LamaYeshe.com

A non-profit charitable organization for the benefit of all
sentient beings and an affiliate of the Foundation for
the Preservation of the Mahayana Tradition
www.fpmt.org

First published in Singapore, 2000
This slightly revised edition published 2006
15,000 copies for free distribution
Second printing 2010, 10,000 copies

Lama Yeshe Wisdom Archive
PO Box 636, Lincoln, MA 01773, USA

Library of Congress Cataloging-in-Publication Data
Thubten Zopa, Rinpoche, 1945-
The joy of compassion / Thubten Zopa, Rinpoche ;
edited by Nicholas Ribush. — Slightly rev. ed.
p. cm.
"First published in Singapore, 2000."
Includes bibliographical references.
Summary: "During the 1999 Vajrasattva Retreat at Land of Medicine Buddha,
California, Lama Zopa Rinpoche gave a series of weekend public talks focusing
mainly on the topic of compassion. This volume contains four of these teachings,
in which Rinpoche really makes clear the importance of the good heart in
Mahayana Buddhism and life in general"—Provided by publisher.
ISBN 978-1-891868-17-7
1. Compassion—Religious aspects—Buddhism. 2. Religious life—Buddhism.
I. Ribush, Nicholas. II. Title.
BQ4360.T49 2006
294.3'5677—dc22
2010029701

10 9 8 7 6 5 4 3 2

Front cover photo by Roger Kunsang • Cover line art by Robert Beer
Designed by Gopa & Ted2 Inc.

♻ Printed in the USA with environmental mindfulness on 30% PCW
recycled paper. As a result we have saved the following resources: 13 trees,
357 lbs. of solid waste, 5,887 gallons of water, 1,222 lbs. of greenhouse gases
and 4 million BTUs of energy. This paper is also FSC certifi ed.
For more information please visit www.fscus.org

Please contact the Lama Yeshe Wisdom Archive
for more copies of this and our other free books

··· Contents ···

· · · Publisher's Acknowledgments · · ·

WE ARE EXTREMELY GRATEFUL to our friends and supporters who have made it possible for the Lama Yeshe Wisdom Archive to both exist and function: to Lama Yeshe and Lama Zopa Rinpoche, whose kindness is impossible to repay; to Peter and Nicole Kedge and Venerable Ailsa Cameron for their initial work on the Archive; to Venerable Roger Kunsang, Lama Zopa's tireless assistant, for his kindness and consideration; and to our sustaining supporters: Barry and Connie Hershey, Joan Halsall, Tony Steel, Vajrayana Institute, Claire Atkins, Thubten Yeshe, Roger and Claire Ash-Wheeler, Hawk Furman, Richard Gere, Lily Chang Wu, Doss McDavid, Therese Miller, Janet Hintermann, Tom and Suzanne Castles, Doren and Mary Harper, and other anonymous benefactors.

We are also deeply grateful to all those who have become members of the Archive over the past few years. Details of our membership program may be found at the back of this book, and if you are not a member, please do consider joining up. Due to the kindness of those who have, we now have several editors working on our vast collection of teachings for the benefit of all. We have posted our list of individual and corporate members on our website, www.LamaYeshe.com.

In particular, I would like to thank those kind supporters who responded to our appeal for funds for this reprint: Alejandra Almada, Chandrakirti Centre, Thubten Pema, Brad Griffith, Sean C. Barrie, Lynda Millspaugh, our anonymous donors and many other generous sponsors.

Furthermore, we would like to express our appreciation for the kindness and compassion of all those other generous benefactors who have contributed funds to our work since we began publishing free books. Thankfully, you are too numerous to mention individually in this book, but we value highly each and every donation made to spreading the Dharma for the sake of the kind mother sentient beings and now pay tribute to you all on our website. Thank you so much.

Finally, I would like to thank the many other kind people who have asked that their donations be kept anonymous; my wife, Wendy Cook, for her constant help and support; our dedicated office staff, Jennifer Barlow and Ven. Ani Tenzin Desal; Ven. Ailsa Cameron for her decades of meticulous editing; Ven. Connie Miller, Gordon McDougall, Michelle Bernard and our other editors; Ven. Kunsang for his tireless work recording Lama Zopa Rinpoche; Ven. Thubten Labdron, Ven. Thubten Munsel and Dr. Su Hung for their help with transcribing; Sandy Smith and our team of volunteer web editors; Ven. Bob Alcorn for his incredible work on our Lama Yeshe DVDs; David Zinn for his digital imaging expertise; Jonathan Steyn for his help with our audio work; Mandala Books and Wisdom Books for their help with our distribution in Australia and Europe and Amitabha Buddhist Centre and Losang Dragpa Centre for their help with our distribution in Singapore and Malaysia respectively; and everybody else who helps us in so many ways. Thank you all.

If you, dear reader, would like to join this noble group of openhearted altruists by contributing to the production of more books by Lama Yeshe or Lama Zopa Rinpoche or to any other aspect of the Lama Yeshe Wisdom Archive's work, please contact us to find out how.

—*Dr. Nicholas Ribush*

Through the merit of having contributed to the spread of the Buddha's
teachings for the sake of all sentient beings, may our benefactors
and their families and friends have long and healthy lives,
all happiness, and may all their Dharma
wishes be instantly fulfilled.

· · · · ·

BENEFACTOR'S DEDICATION

To our parents, for this precious human rebirth.
To our Gurus, for their limitless patience and kindness,
and tireless teaching.
By this merit, may we always go for refuge to our Gurus and
the Three Jewels; with the mind of enlightenment and wisdom,
be only causes of happiness for all sentient beings.
By this merit until samsara ends, please, our precious Gurus,
stay with us, and lead us to the bliss of complete Buddhahood.

··· Editor's Preface ···

I N THIS BOOK, Lama Zopa Rinpoche emphasizes one of his favorite themes, compassion, and how the purpose of our lives is to strive for the benefit of others. Living with compassion not only helps others; it helps us as well. In fact, if we want the best for ourselves, we should dedicate ourselves completely to the welfare of others, putting their happiness first and our own last—an attitude that His Holiness the Dalai Lama describes as "wise selfishness."

The teachings in this book have been drawn from Lama Zopa Rinpoche's extensive, 700-page work, *Teachings from the Vajrasattva Retreat*, teachings given at a three-month retreat held at the FPMT Center, Land of Medicine Buddha, California, in 1999. As a result, there are more references to Vajrasattva practice and other practices than might otherwise have been expected, but the points Rinpoche makes have universal applicability and should be taken in that way.

I would like to thank my co-editor of the Vajrasattva retreat book, Venerable Ailsa Cameron, and all the other people who helped put it together, and Wendy Cook for her valuable editorial comments.

Deer Park, Wisconsin, 2008

· · · 1 · · ·

Living with Compassion

WHAT IS IT that makes your life easy and free of confusion and problems? What is the source of all happiness and peace? What brings happiness and peace into your daily life and all happiness up to enlightenment, allowing you to bring happiness and peace to numberless sentient beings? It's your attitude—the unmistaken attitude with which you live your life, the attitude by which you live your life according to its meaning, fulfilling your purpose of having been born human.

What is that best attitude that gives the most meaning to your life? It is living with compassion, for the benefit of others.

When your attitude is that of simply seeking your own happiness, the attitude itself attracts many difficulties and creates obstacles to your own success. Even if you are trying to serve others, when your basic motivation is that of seeking your own happiness, you experience many ego clashes and personality problems in trying to work with other people. Whether you are working in a meditation center or an office, if you are self-centered, you will bring all kinds of useless garbage into your life, especially when associating or dealing with others. All kinds of emotional problems will arise.

So even though the work you are doing—working for the welfare of others—is good, your self-centered mind generates all sorts of harmful, unnecessary emotional thoughts—thoughts that are totally useless as far as your job is concerned; thoughts that make others unhappy and angry and disturb their minds. Thoughts such as anger and jealousy create much disharmony between yourself and others. These harmful emotions impede the success of your work, bring no peace, happiness or harmony, interfere with your work and your health, and can even create obstacles to your life, to your very survival. By leading you to suicide, such thoughts can even cause your death—you're not killed by someone else; you're killed by your own emotional mind.

The moment you begin to cherish yourself is the moment you have created an obstacle to success in working for others. Self-cherishing brings constant problems. Broadly speaking, if you have self-cherishing, you cannot develop bodhicitta. As long as you do not renounce self-cherishing, you cannot develop the holy mind of cherishing others. That means you cannot attain enlightenment, cannot work perfectly for the sake of all the numberless sentient beings.

Thus you can see how the self-centered mind is the main obstacle that prevents you from benefiting others. It is from the self-centered mind that desire, anger and all other negative, emotional thoughts arise, obscuring your mind, blocking your wisdom. Even though there may exist many methods for solving a particular problem and you have the potential to apply them, your self-cherishing attitude totally obstructs your wisdom and prevents you from either seeing or applying them. These emotional thoughts obscure your mind and cause it to hallucinate. Therefore, you cannot perceive the methods that would bring happiness, peace and harmony. Even though, simply by changing your attitude—something that your mind is quite capable of doing—you could apply those methods and solve your problems very easily, somehow you never see it or are unable to do it.

Also, when you are not clear about the purpose of life, you are never clear when it comes to making decisions that affect your life. You always hesitate and are always in danger of making the wrong decision. When your only purpose for living is the benefit of others, it is very easy to make the right decision. It is easy because you are very clear about why you are alive.

If there is compassion in your heart, you do not harm others. All other sentient beings receive no harm from you, the one, individual person. Instead of receiving harm from you, they receive peace and happiness. Not only do you not harm them but, out of compassion and according to your ability, you benefit them as much as you can. On the basis of not harming, you benefit. Therefore, numberless sentient beings receive much peace and happiness from your compassion.

So, whether or not numberless sentient beings receive that great peace and happiness is entirely up to you. Giving great peace and happiness to others is completely up to you because it depends upon what you do with your mind, whether or not you practice compassion towards others. Your own mind makes the decision—either you keep going from life to life harming sentient beings directly or indirectly, or you change your attitude from ego to compassion and offer sentient beings all peace and happiness up to enlightenment. All this depends completely on what you do with your own mind.

Therefore, each of us is responsible for the peace and happiness of all sentient beings, of each sentient being—all happiness up to that of enlightenment.

The purpose of our lives is, on the basis of abstaining from harm, to bring happiness to others, to be useful for others, to free them from all suffering and bring them all happiness. One kind of happiness is the happiness of this life, but long-term happiness—happiness in all future lives—is much more important than that. And, while causing others to experience happiness in all future lives is highly meaningful, it is even more important to lead them to the everlasting happiness of total liberation—cessation of the entire round of suffering and its causes, delusion and karma. This is more important than simply the long-term happiness of future lives because the happiness of future lives is still contaminated happiness while the happiness of liberation never diminishes or degenerates. It is the complete cessation of suffering and its causes. Once the seed, or imprint, of delusion has been eradicated, there is no cause for delusion, and therefore suffering, to ever arise again.

However, as important as leading all sentient beings to everlasting happiness might be, the most important thing you can do is to bring them all into the peerless happiness of full enlightenment—the cessation of even the subtle defilements of mind, and the completion of all realizations. However, saying that bringing others to enlightenment is the most important thing does not mean that you should not try to give others the happiness of this life. It means that starting from the intention of enlightening all sentient beings, according to your own ability, you should offer whatever service you possibly can to all other sentient beings. In other words, on the basis of bringing the happiness of this life to others, you lead them to the ultimate happiness of full enlightenment. Or, on the basis of offering others the greatest benefit possible, that of bringing them to enlightenment, you also offer whatever you can of those previous services.

How to attain enlightenment

In order to be able to do perfect work for the numberless other sentient beings, eliminate all their sufferings and lead them from happiness to happiness to full enlightenment, first you have to achieve the omniscient mind of enlightenment yourself. How do you achieve enlightenment? It doesn't happen without cause or by practicing the wrong cause, by following the wrong path. Nor does it happen if you practice an unmistaken method incompletely, for example, spending your entire life—twenty, thirty, forty, fifty . . . eighty, ninety years of life—just doing breathing meditation. Even though breathing meditation is recommended as a tool to calm your mind and might be useful for developing single-pointed concentration and making your mind peaceful, that alone does not get you anywhere, does not transform your mind into virtue or diminish or eradicate delusions.

To terminate delusions, you need to realize emptiness; to eradicate ignorance, the root, or cause, of all the delusions, you have to realize emptiness. So how can you do that just by practicing breathing meditation? How can you escape from samsara by spending your whole life watching your breath? There's no way. Spending your entire life practicing mindfulness of the body, watching your abdomen rise and fall—after you've eaten a big meal or when your belly is empty! Anyway, I'm joking.

Spending your whole life developing awareness of your bodily sen-

sations might help you prevent strong anger or strong desire from arising at the time, but even if you spend your whole life with your mind
watching your mind, your mind meditating on your mind, if you meditate on only the conventional nature of mind and not its ultimate
nature, if you simply practice single-pointed concentration on the conventional nature of mind, how can that stop ignorance? How can that
cut the root of samsara? There's no way.

Spending your time doing that is like trying to stop a poisonous plant
from growing by planting another one next to it. It's like trying to
destroy a poisonous plant by putting cotton wool alongside it. Even if
you spend your whole life practicing mind concentrating on mind, how
can that eradicate the root of samsara, the concept of the inherently-
existent I, the inherently-existent aggregates? It's impossible. It would
not affect that one bit; it would not do anything.

The root of samsara is the perverted mind [Tib. *log-she*]. Although
there is no I on the aggregates—not even a merely labeled I on the base,
the aggregates—as soon as the I is merely labeled by the mind, it appears
to our hallucinating mind as if it is, in fact, on the aggregates—like a
brocade tablecloth covering a table or a book lying on a table. You see
that it is *there* on the aggregates, which is the same as saying that the I
appears from its own side; the merely labeled I, the I that is merely
labeled by your mind, appears back to your mind, your hallucinating
mind, as if it exists from its own side. Then you allow your mind to
believe that it is true; you allow your mind to hold on to that inherently-
existent I. That concept is *log-she*, the totally perverted mind, the totally
wrong concept, the totally hallucinating mind, and the *only way* to eliminate it is to recognize what it is that the concept is holding on to, to

recognize the way this concept apprehends the I.

When you *don't* investigate, it looks like it's there, but when you examine it more closely you see that it is not there. While your mind is unaware, not analyzing, it looks as if it's there, but when your mind investigates, it cannot be found either on the aggregates or anywhere else. It is totally non-existent.

Even though you cannot find the merely labeled I on the base, on the aggregates, you can find it where the aggregates are. Where there is the base, there you will find the merely labeled I. You just can't find it *on* the base.

The object that this ignorance, the root of samsara, the concept of inherent existence, apprehends, what it holds onto, cannot be found either on the aggregates or anywhere else. It is totally non-existent; it has *never* existed since beginningless time. From beginningless rebirths, the inherently existent I has never existed; it doesn't exist now and it has never existed.

All buddhas realize that there is no inherently existent I, even though the merely labeled I, merely labeled actions, merely labeled objects, merely labeled hell, merely labeled enlightenment, merely labeled path, merely labeled samsara, merely labeled nirvana, merely labeled happiness, merely labeled suffering, merely labeled virtue, merely labeled non-virtue—which in reality exist merely in name and are completely empty of inherent existence—are covered by our hallucinating view with the appearance of inherent existence.

Our hallucinating view covers everything—the merely labeled I, merely labeled actions, merely labeled objects, merely labeled enemies, merely labeled friends, merely labeled money, merely labeled jobs, the whole thing—all phenomena, which exist in mere name and are empty of inherent existence, with the appearance of inherent existence. This is how it is; this is our world. But what the numberless buddhas and bodhisattvas who have realized emptiness see is that all these appearances are completely non-existent; that there is not the slightest atom of inherent existence anywhere.

So, to go back to what I was saying before, even if you spend your entire life watching your mind, single-pointedly concentrating on your mind, that alone will not have the slightest effect on the root of samsara. It will give no harm to your ignorance; your ignorance will remain very comfortable, with its entourage of delusions very well established. That kind of meditation alone can never help liberate you from samsara; it does nothing.

To make it impossible for delusions to arise, you have to eradicate their seed. To prevent the cause of samsara, delusion and karma, from ever arising, to make sure that ignorance, attachment and anger never arise at all, ever again, you have to eradicate the seed of delusion, which is in the nature of imprints on the continuity of your consciousness, according to the Prasangika school of Buddhist philosophy, the merely labeled I. Only by realizing emptiness, by developing the wisdom that directly perceives emptiness, can you eradicate the seed of delusion. Nothing else can directly do this.

Therefore, if you spend your entire life just doing breathing meditation—or even "mind concentrating on mind" meditation, which has nothing to do with the ultimate nature of mind—you cannot remove the seed of delusion or put a final end to the delusions, and you certainly can't reach enlightenment. That's totally out of the question.

In order to attain enlightenment, you have to practice all the methods without exception. Not only that, you have to practice these methods in the right order, without mixing them up. If you practice them out of order you cannot attain enlightenment. To reach full enlightenment, to actualize the *lam-rim*, the steps of the path to enlightenment, you have to actualize the graduated path of the practitioner of highest capability. Doing that depends upon your having actualized as a foundation the graduated path of the practitioner of intermediate capability. That in turn depends upon your having prepared by actualizing the graduated path of the practitioner of least capability.

Guru devotion

In order to actualize the graduated path of the practitioner of least capability, you need—as Lama Tsong Khapa mentions in his short lam-rim text, *The Foundation of All Good Qualities*—to see that correct devotion to the kind guru, who is the foundation of all good qualities, is the root of the path.[1] That is the foundation of all realizations, from that of the perfect human rebirth and the graduated path of the practitioner of least capability all the way up to enlightenment. It is not only the foundation of all realizations—it is also the foundation of every good thing that ever happens in your life, of any happiness that you ever experience: in past lives, in this life, and in all future lives up to enlightenment. Every good thing, every single happiness, comes from that field that is the guru. Therefore, correct devotion to your guru is the root of

---

[1] See Appendix 1

the path.

The text continues: "By clearly seeing this and applying great effort, please bless me to rely upon him with great respect."

The words "great effort" have deep significance. What Lama Tsong Khapa is saying here is that seeing your virtuous friend as pure, as buddha, has to come with much effort from your own side. Seeing your guru as buddha doesn't come from his side, independently. It has to come from your own side, and with much effort. Seeing him as pure takes much, continual effort. Seeing him as pure, as having eradicated all the errors of mind and possessing all good qualities, takes not just a few days, not just an hour's meditation, not just two or three months of meditation, but year upon year, life upon life, of effort. This is how much effort it takes to be able to practice guru devotion correctly with thought and action. That's what this teaching means. Not just a few minutes' practice, then stop; an hour's practice, then stop; a year's practice, then stop. Not like that.

In the *Lam-rim Chen-mo*, Lama Tsong Khapa explains nine attitudes of guru devotion; nine attitudes to have when correctly devoting yourself to your guru.[2] If you read those you can get an idea of the right way to practice guru devotion, the root of the path.

The perfect human rebirth

In the second verse of *The Foundation of All Good Qualities*, Lama Tsong Khapa mentions that on the basis of correct guru devotion, you should

---

[2] See Appendix 2

understand that this time not only have you found a precious human body, which in itself is extremely rare, but one that is qualified by eight freedoms and ten richnesses, which is much more rare. And specifically, at this time you have met the precious Buddhadharma and a virtuous friend revealing not only the unmistaken path but also the complete path, with nothing missing. Therefore, you have every opportunity to practice all the steps of the entire path to enlightenment. This is what you have received, just this once.

When you are born in the hell realm, you encounter every possible obstacle. This time, you have received every opportunity to practice Dharma. Whatever happiness you want—any great meaning of this life, the happiness of future lives, liberation from samsara, the full enlightenment of buddhahood—whichever of these you want, you can achieve with this present perfect human body. What you want is happiness; what you don't want is suffering. With this highly meaningful perfect human body, you can abandon all the causes of suffering and create all the causes of happiness, because all suffering comes only from non-virtue and all happiness comes only from virtue, only from Dharma. As Nagarjuna explained, actions born from attachment, anger and ignorance are non-virtuous—from those, all suffering transmigrators arise—whereas actions born from non-attachment, non-anger and non-ignorance are virtuous—from those, all happy transmigrators arise.

Therefore, what you should do is practice only Dharma, nothing else, because happiness is all you want. Since that is your wish, you should create only virtue, you should practice only Dharma. Not only that, but you must practice Dharma in this life. You cannot leave it for future lives because it will be extremely difficult to find such an opportunity again. After this life it will be almost impossible to receive as perfect a human body as the one you have now, with which you can achieve all the different levels of happiness beyond this life—the happiness of future lives, liberation from samsara and full enlightenment. With this body, you can achieve whatever you want, but you have found it only this once and such a body will be extremely difficult to find again in the future.

Impermanence and death

Not only should you practice Dharma in this life but you should also practice it right now. Not only is death certain but it can also come at any time, even today, even at this very moment. Therefore you should practice Dharma right now. Moreover, you should practice only Dharma, because at the time of death nothing else will help. You have to leave behind your entire family and even your own body, which, of all sentient beings' bodies, is the one you have cherished the most. No matter how many friends or how much wealth you have, nothing can be carried into your future lives. Naked, your consciousness goes alone into your next life. As many lamas have mentioned in their lam-rim teachings, when you pull a hair from butter, it slips out with no butter attached. Like that, your bare consciousness will go alone into the next life. Therefore, at the time of death, nothing other than Buddhadharma can be of benefit. Furthermore, only Dharma can benefit your next life and those beyond. Therefore, practice Dharma and only Dharma.

In his teachings, Lama Tsong Khapa says that at the time of death, nothing other than the holy Dharma can be of benefit. There are three things to think. When you see you have to go to the next life, away from this life, away from this world, even if at the time of death you are surrounded by your relatives and friends, no matter how much they love you, how much affection they have for you, none of them can go with you. And no matter how much wealth you possess, how many piles of beautiful objects you have, you can't take even an atom with you. Finally, you have to leave behind even the flesh and bone with which you were born. If you have to leave even your flesh and bones, there's no question that you will also have to leave behind the other perfections of this life. Therefore, you should think, "It is certain that I will pass to another world and when that happens I will have to leave all this behind." Moreover, you should think that this will happen today and that at death, *only* the Dharma will be your savior, refuge and guide.

Lama Tsong Khapa refers to a quotation from the writings of Karni-karnika, who says, "When the view of the ripening aspect result of previous karma arises and the Lord of Death invites migratory beings to follow their new karma, they have to leave behind everything but their negative karma and virtue; nobody comes along with them. Understand this and practice well."

Thus Lama Tsong Khapa emphasizes that leisure has great significance, is extremely difficult to find and decays very easily, so remember death. He says if you don't try to achieve happiness beyond this life, even though you have received a human rebirth, it's as if you have not and your life has no more meaning than that of an animal. As far as achieving happiness and avoiding suffering up until the time of death are concerned—in other words, attaining the happiness of this life and solving this life's problems—Lama Tsong Khapa says that animals are even better at it than humans. However, we should conduct ourselves better than animals do. Since being born human is special, our conduct should surpass that of animals. Otherwise, Lama Tsong Khapa says, even though you have achieved the body of a happy transmigrator, it's as if you have not.

If you lead your life no better than an animal, if your attitude is simply that of seeking your own happiness of this life, no matter how successful you might be in achieving it, your life is no more special than that of an animal. No matter how powerful or famous you become—or whatever other happiness of this life you seek—your attitude and conduct is no better than that of an animal. If this is how you live your life, your having achieved this human body has no meaning.

In his *Guide to the Bodhisattva's Way of Life*, Shantideva says, "It is not rare for animals to engage in meaningless activities, but freedom and richness, which are extremely difficult to find, are destroyed by those tormented by karma."[3]

I'm not one hundred percent sure, but my guess is that he means that insignificant or meaningless activities are not hard to create; even animals can do those well. But if we use our perfect human rebirth, which will be so difficult to find again, for creating negative karma by engaging in meaningless activity instead of using it to achieve the happiness beyond this life all the way up to enlightenment, we are destroying the rare and precious opportunity we have. If, instead of creating good karma, the cause of all happiness, we use our perfect human body to create negative karma, all these good results—good rebirths, liberation

---

[3] Chapter 8, verse 81

from samsara, enlightenment—are destroyed and we will have to experience rebirth in the lower realms.

I think this is what Shantideva means by "destroy." For example, when you get angry, the anger destroys your liberation. How? By destroying your merits. Because anger destroys your merits, anger destroys your liberation. Shantideva's meaning might be similar to that. If, with this perfect human rebirth and that kind of attitude you create negative karma, you will experience only suffering rebirths and will not achieve all those good rebirths, from better future lives all the way up to enlightenment. It's like the negative karma destroyed all those good results. I think that's what it means.

From the holy mouth of the Kadampa Geshe Potowa: "Your main practice should be meditation on impermanence in order to eliminate the appearance of this life. Eliminate the appearance of this life, your family, relatives, possessions and so forth, knowing that you yourself must go from this life unaccompanied, alone, and that nothing but Dharma can help you at that time. Thinking in this way, live without attachment to this life. Until this thought arises in your mind, your entire Dharma path is blocked."

Geshe Potowa is saying that until the thought of impermanence and death arises in your mind—the thought that death can come at any moment and that at the time of death none of the perfections or activities of this life can be of benefit and you have to go alone into the next life—and you have developed detachment from this life, the entire path of Dharma is blocked.

In other words, the concept of permanence, the attachment clinging to this life, the thought, "I am going to live for a long time," which is opposite to the thought of impermanence and death, blocks the path of the entire Dharma. First of all, it prevents your mind from becoming Dharma; it does not allow your daily attitude to become Dharma. This prevents all your actions from becoming Dharma; therefore, they all become non-virtuous. That is the immediate obstacle—your attitude of mind in daily life not becoming Dharma and as a result, all your actions not becoming Dharma actions.

Therefore you cannot gain the realizations of the graduated path of the practitioner of least capability, those of the graduated path of the practitioner of intermediate capability or those of the graduated path of the practitioner of highest capability. Since you have no renunciation of this life, no renunciation of future lives in samsara, you cannot achieve the graduated path of the practitioner of intermediate capability, which is the foundation. Similarly, you cannot achieve the graduated path of the practitioner of highest capability, bodhicitta or the rest of the Mahayana path. Therefore, you cannot receive enlightenment. That's the meaning of the entire Dharma path being blocked.

Kadampa Geshe Torwa said, "If, by the way, you practice precisely, try to collect merits and purify your defilements with effort and zeal, and make requests to the guru and the deity, even though you think you won't attain any realizations for a hundred years, since causative phenomena cannot remain static, realizations will come."

What he is saying is that if you practice whole-heartedly, correctly, with effort and precision; if, while you are meditating on the path, you also constantly, from the bottom of your heart, pray, make single-pointed requests to the guru-deity; if you continue to practice like this, even though you might think that you will never gain any realizations, such as those of emptiness, bodhicitta, renunciation or tantra, even though you think, "Oh, how could it possibly happen? Poor me! I'm this and that . . . how could someone like me attain realizations? It will take ages, a hundred years," even though that's what you believe about your gaining realizations, because of all the practices you do and because your mind is a causative phenomenon—it exists through dependence upon causes and conditions—without choice, your mind has to change. It cannot stay as it is. Your mind cannot remain in its old, hard state; it has to change. That's what Geshe Torwa is saying—realizations can happen very easily, without taking a hundred years.

In the quotation above, "by the way" could mean while you are meditating on the path, training your mind in the lam-rim, or it could mean trying to use even your daily activities—eating, sleeping, washing and so forth—as a means of collecting extensive merits and purifying defilements. "By the way" could mean either of those things.

Lam-rim and retreat

I just want to make a few points about the place of lam-rim practice in deity retreat. To help any retreat we are doing become a stronger, more powerful purification, to increase our determination to practice Dharma so that we can defeat the delusions, overcome the obstacles that prevent us from achieving enlightenment—the self-cherishing thought and so forth—and to strengthen our minds so that we can overcome our inner obstacles, which prevent us from freeing ourselves from samsara, we should always remember and meditate on the teachings of the lam-rim, the graduated path to enlightenment.

Getting free from samsara or remaining trapped within it depends entirely on which is stronger, the delusions or the mind. It's a question of this. If our mind becomes stronger than our delusions, we'll get free from samsara. If we allow our mind to be weak and our delusions to be strong, if we give freedom to our delusions instead of ourselves, we will not find liberation, only more samsaric suffering.

The conclusion is this. Not all of us can live ascetic lives in isolated places, but we all have to practice Dharma as much as possible. There's no choice. Therefore, we have to remember impermanence and death as much as we possibly can, since this is the mind that serves as a remedy to the attachment clinging to this life. This attachment is what brings us all our problems, confusion and obstacles to Dharma practice. It prevents our attitude and actions from becoming Dharma and prevents the Dharma that we do practice from becoming pure. Meditation on impermanence and death must become our fundamental weapon, our main remedy, or antidote, to the delusions.

The incredible power of bodhicitta

On the basis of this, we should generate the good heart, bodhicitta, the thought of benefiting others. This is our best refuge, especially for those of us whose lives are very busy, who don't have much time for sitting or other traditional forms of practice. On the basis of reflecting on impermanence and death, we should make the good heart the main object of refuge in our lives. This allows all our actions to become Dharma, the cause of enlightenment and the cause of happiness for all sentient beings. Therefore, we should lead our lives with this attitude, the thought of benefiting all sentient beings.

If you recite a Vajrasattva mantra once with bodhicitta you get the same benefit as you do from reciting 100,000 without it. If you make one light offering with bodhicitta, you get the same amount of merit as you do from making 100,000 light offerings without it. If you make charity of one dollar to a sentient being—a beggar or a homeless person—with bodhicitta, you get the same amount of merit as you do from making charity of $100,000 without it.

It is said in the scriptures that if the sentient beings of three galaxies—the Tibetan term is *tong-sum*, but I'm not exactly sure how best to translate it, you should check for yourselves—all build stupas of the seven precious substances, such as gold, diamonds and so forth, and fill the whole world with these stupas, the merit of that is far less than that created by just one person offering a tiny flower to the Buddha with bodhicitta motivation. The person making this small offering with bodhicitta motivation creates far more merit than three galaxies of sentient beings covering the world with stupas made of the seven precious substances without it.

Try to imagine this. If you build just one stupa you create unbelievable merit. It directs your life to enlightenment and is an amazing purification. So here we have three galaxies' worth of sentient beings, each one building a stupa of the seven precious substances—not with bricks and mortar but with precious jewels—and covering the world with these. Nevertheless, the merit of one person offering a tiny flower to the Buddha with bodhicitta motivation creates far more merit than that.

Thinking about this should inspire you to make bodhicitta your heart practice. It transforms your life like iron into gold or kaka into diamonds. Bodhicitta motivation gives your life its greatest possible meaning and makes every single action of your daily life as beneficial as it can possibly be. You should remember bodhicitta from morning to night, twenty-four hours a day. Hold it as your most precious possession, as your wish-fulfilling jewel. You should cherish your bodhicitta motivation above all else; remember it constantly and practice it at every moment.

If you do one prostration with bodhicitta, it's as if you did 100,000 prostrations. In *Liberation in the Palm of Your Hand*, Pabongka Dechen Nyingpo explains that if you recite the "Praises to the Twenty-one Taras" once with bodhicitta you get the benefit of having recited it 100,000 times. Hence, if you do pujas or recite prayers for others with bodhicitta they become much more powerful and create far more merit.

Therefore the amount of purification you get from a Vajrasattva retreat doesn't depend upon how many mantras you recite but on their quality. Of course, the number has power, but the quality of your recitation is much more important. So even if you recite just one Vajrasattva mantra, how much negative karma gets purified depends on how you recite it. Therefore, when you do your motivation you should meditate very precisely on the lam-rim, especially bodhicitta, and generate regret.

The power of regret

Ordinary people might think that regretting mistaken actions is negative thinking but people who are practitioners, who have faith in the

Buddha's teachings and the lam-rim and have been practicing deeply, see it as positive. Beginners, too, might think that generating the thought of regret is negative. But if you understand the Dharma—especially Mahayana practices such as the Thirty-five Buddhas practice, where you recite the names of those extremely powerful buddhas, and, in particular, the skillful methods of Highest Yoga Tantra, such as the practice of the Highest Yoga Tantra aspect of Vajrasattva—your regret serves as medicine; it heals you.

The lam-rim teachings cite six methods of purification. Practicing Vajrasattva, for example, with your knowledge of Buddhadharma, especially the powerful purification methods of the skillful means of tantra, your regret becomes a technique of healing. It purifies your negative karma so that you avoid obstacles and don't have to experience its suffering result, and even if you do, the experience is either very light or delayed for a long time; many lifetimes, even eons. Thus, the generation of regret heals, purifies negative karma, and brings happiness and peace, not only in this life but in all lives, from now to enlightenment.

Even if you don't do these methods of purification—Vajrasattva, prostrations to the Thirty-five Buddhas while reciting their names, making tsa-tsas and statues of buddhas and so forth—just feeling regret for the negative karmas you have created or for the harm you have given others lightens that negative karma. The stronger the regret, the lighter the negative karma becomes. Therefore, feeling regret is positive—it's healing; it's purification. Generating regret is the path to happiness, even though at the time it might feel unpleasant. Never mind; it has a good future! When you tally your negative karmas, count them one by one, make an account of them, you might not feel so good, but that feeling of regret has a good future because it purifies them; at least, it makes them lighter and shorter. Thus, it is positive.

Therefore, it is wrong to think that just because at the moment something feels unpleasant it must be negative. That kind of thinking becomes an obstacle to purifying your negative karma, to avoiding your future suffering, to freeing yourself from samsara, to attaining enlightenment, to achieving realizations. Instead of focusing on the incredible benefits you'll gain, all that future peace and happiness, interpreting the whole thing as negative becomes a huge block to all those good results.

A similar thing can happen when you don't know how to think about impermanence and death properly. If you don't know Dharma or don't practice, thinking about impermanence and death can be like torturing yourself because you don't have a solution to the problem. But if you know Dharma, and especially if you practice, then instead of becoming unpleasant, thinking about impermanence and death can become incredibly beneficial. You can overcome all your delusions, you can begin to practice Dharma without obstacles, you can continue to practice without obstacles, and you can complete your practice without obstacles and attain enlightenment. These are some of the benefits, as mentioned in the lam-rim teachings. If you practice Dharma, you receive these benefits, but if you don't, then thinking of death just makes you unhappy.

If you practice Dharma, thinking about impermanence and death allows you to overcome death itself. When you start to meditate on impermanence and death, you are afraid of death, but this fear makes you practice Dharma. Then, through practicing Dharma, you gain the realizations of renunciation of samsara, bodhicitta and emptiness, and in that way gradually overcome your fear of death. Eventually, you become free of even death itself. As Milarepa said, "Afraid of death, I fled to the mountains, where I realized the ultimate nature of the primordial mind. Now, even should I die, I'll be unafraid."

In that way, Dharma practitioners think about impermanence and death, which spurs them on to develop their practice until they have overcome not only the fear of death, but death itself.

Lama Zopa Rinpoche gave this teaching 13 February 1999.

Deer Park, Wisconsin, 2008

2

Getting the Best from Your Life

WHAT MAKES YOUR LIFE most beautiful, most satisfying, most fulfilling, most worthwhile, most beneficial and most happy? I mean inner happiness, not just ordinary, excited, hallucinated happiness. What brings Dharma happiness, the happiness that has completion, the happiness that can continue, increase and develop fully? The happiness that is not suffering, that is worth trying for because it never turns into suffering? The happiness that is not suffering in nature and does not become the suffering of pain? Dharma happiness, the happiness that is worth devoting your life to attaining because it does not interfere with the happiness of others or limit your capacity to benefit others? The happiness that makes your actions only of benefit to others without discrimination?

Well, so far I've been doing a lot of advertising but I haven't mentioned the product! So, what is it? It's living in the bush—going into the redwoods and living in the bush! No, I'm joking! So, what is it that brings all that happiness? It's cherishing sentient beings; living your life cherishing sentient beings. Not that I actually do this myself, but intellectually, it's what I think. Cherish sentient beings first; put enlightenment second.

Sentient beings come first

Why do I say put enlightenment second? For example, when you go into the kitchen, you're looking for food, not crockery; your motivation is not to get a plate but delicious food. You go into the kitchen with food on your mind. But although your main motivation is to get food, you do need something to put it on—unless you can carry soup in your hands! Anyway, I'm joking again.

Of course, enlightenment is extremely important because without it you cannot work perfectly for sentient beings. You cannot be a perfect guide, knowing, seeing directly, every sentient being's mind, level of karma, intelligence, wishes and characteristics, as well as the various methods that suit their individual dispositions. But what should be in your heart is sentient beings as the reason for your attaining enlightenment. The first priority in your heart should be the happiness of sentient beings; sentient beings in your heart. What should be the first thing in your heart, in your life, the goal of your life? Sentient beings.

At present, who is the most precious person in your life, in your heart? It's yourself or, if not yourself, then your greatest object of attachment. I don't think you hold your object of anger most precious. It's your object of attachment; that particular person. So that's how you should hold sentient beings, feel them to be most precious.

No matter how much you help the person to whom you are most attached, no matter how kind you are to that person, all you want is for *that* person to be happy. If that person receives help, achieves happiness, you're satisfied. That's your goal; you don't want anything in return. You don't need that person to respect you, to praise you or to do something good for you in return; you don't have any such expectation. Your attitude is such that you are simply satisfied by that person's receiving happiness or help. What do you call it—unconditional love? Anyway, that kind of attitude, whether it's all sentient beings or one sentient being.

First in your heart, your first priority, at least intellectually, should be all sentient beings. Then, enlightenment is the method. As in the example above, to enjoy food you need a plate on which to put it. When you're looking for lunch, you're not looking for the plate; your main aim is the food. So here, what we're really looking for is the happiness of sentient beings.

Although you might be thinking, "I'm working for enlightenment, practicing Dharma, doing retreat to attain enlightenment," sometimes you can make the mistake of leaving one particular sentient being out. Even though your enlightenment depends upon that sentient being's kindness, you leave that sentient being out; you give that sentient being up as an object of compassion or loving kindness. That sentient being becomes the object of your anger. You say, "I'm meditating to reach enlightenment," but you use that sentient being who gives you enlightenment as an object of anger—to hurt, to give harm. You treat that person as useless, worse than garbage.

If you have that kind of attitude, it's not sure that your thought of seeking enlightenment is actual bodhicitta or not. Even though you use the term "enlightenment," perhaps it's just your self-centered mind wanting to attain the highest possible level of happiness for yourself. The essence, the very heart of your attitude, what's really deep within, is the wish to experience the highest happiness yourself. It's possible for this to happen.

Generally speaking, as much as you think it's important to attain enlightenment, equally you should be thinking that other sentient beings are important, precious, so precious, the most precious thing in your life. Such thoughts should always accompany your thoughts of enlightenment.

In the process of developing bodhicitta we often use the seven techniques of Mahayana cause and effect. And on the basis of renunciation of this life and renunciation of samsara, we equalize ourselves with and exchange ourselves for others. With effort, we generate the feeling of the preciousness of other sentient beings and then the need to achieve enlightenment ourselves in order to accomplish the aims of others, to fulfill others' wishes for happiness. This is the usual process.

The mistake is to think of attaining enlightenment but not taking care of sentient beings, giving them up. Who gives you enlightenment? Upon whose kindness do you depend in order to achieve it? And then you don't take care of them, renounce them, pay them no attention? Instead of treating sentient beings with kindness, compassion and patience, you use them as objects of anger, to give rise to delusions.

Because parents cherish their children most in their lives, if you harm the children you also harm their parents. In general, parents cherish the health, well-being and long lives of their children more than their own. Therefore, if you cherish sentient beings, you are naturally serving and pleasing the numberless buddhas and bodhisattvas; your serving and benefiting sentient beings makes numberless buddhas and bodhisattvas happy. Perhaps not in every case, but generally speaking, by making sentient beings happy, you also make the buddhas and bodhisattvas happy. Generally, this can be said, but I wouldn't say that this is true in every situation. Thinking that it is could lead you to make big mistakes in your life.

However, offering service to sentient beings is the best offering of service to the buddhas and bodhisattvas; making offerings to sentient beings is the best way of making offerings to the buddhas and bodhisattvas; serving sentient beings is the best offering you can make to the buddhas and bodhisattvas. This doesn't mean that you should stop making offerings to the buddhas and bodhisattvas: "Oh, I'm serving sentient beings, I don't need to do other practices"—like prostrations, mandala offerings, other offerings, the seven-limb practice and so forth—practices that are recommended for attaining realizations on the path to enlightenment. That, too, is mistaken.

Easy merit

Actually, because of the power of the object, the easiest way of creating good karma, the easiest way of attaining enlightenment, is with holy objects—Buddha, Dharma and Sangha; statues, stupas and scriptures. Normally we need to generate bodhicitta motivation for our actions— working, walking, sitting, sleeping and so forth—to become the cause of enlightenment. Even for these actions to become the cause of our own liberation, we need to generate renunciation of samsara. And for them to become simply the cause of happiness in future lives, samsaric happiness, even for that we need renunciation of this life; we have to create pure, Dharma actions with a mind detached from the happiness of this life. Forget about renunciation of samsara and bodhicitta, even to have the constant thought of renunciation of this life, to maintain a pure mind, twenty-four hours a day is not easy.

But because of the power of the holy object, such as statues of buddha, stupas and scriptures, buddha's kindness and compassion for us sentient beings, and the inconceivable qualities that buddha has attained, just by circumambulating or prostrating or making offerings to these symbolic holy objects, we can immediately create the causes for enlightenment, liberation and better rebirths. Even if our mind is not one of the three principal paths—I don't mean the actual realization, but even if it's not one of the artificial three principal paths, the motivation generated through the effort of thinking about the benefits of achieving enlightenment and wanting to attain it, or of meditating on how the nature of samsara is suffering and arousing detachment—even if our mind has no Dharma motivation at all and is completely non-virtuous, even with that attitude, because of buddha's incredible compassion for us sentient beings and his inconceivable qualities, by doing those actions we can create the good karma, the merit, for liberation and enlightenment and, by the way, good rebirths in hundreds or thousands of future lives, and experience all happiness and success in this life too.

However, the purpose of collecting such extensive merit by making offerings to Buddha, Dharma and Sangha, statues, stupas and scriptures is to be able to dedicate it to the happiness and well-being of other sentient beings. You create this powerful merit, this strong karma, and then dedicate it, use it, to accomplish the aims of numberless other sentient beings, to bring happiness to other sentient beings—the happiness of this life, of future lives, of liberation from samsara and the highest, full enlightenment.

Enlightenment comes from sentient beings

As Shantideva said in his *Guide to the Bodhisattva's Way of Life*, "Since we achieve the Dharma by depending equally on the buddhas and sentient beings, why shouldn't we respect sentient beings as much as we respect the buddhas?"[4]

Guru Shakyamuni Buddha gave teachings on patience, giving us the opportunity to practice patience. He taught us how to follow the path to enlightenment, how to eradicate our defilements, and how to liberate ourselves from the suffering of samsara by revealing the path, by revealing the teachings. Therefore we think that he is so precious, so kind. However, sentient beings are equally so. Even though it was the Buddha who revealed the teachings, without the existence of sentient beings, without that sentient being who is angry at you, how can you learn to be patient, how can you realize the perfection of patience? Without that being you cannot complete the paramita of patience, you cannot attain enlightenment.

Even through this example, you can see how it is equal. Buddha gives you enlightenment by revealing the path, by giving teachings, by showing you how to practice patience. Similarly, the sentient being who is angry at you gives you enlightenment by giving you the opportunity of putting these teachings of the Buddha into practice. Therefore, just as the Buddha is kind and precious, so too is that sentient being.

The same thing applies to the entire path to enlightenment taught by the Buddha. Actualizing this path depends on the kindness of sentient

---

[4] Chapter 6, verse 113

beings. Without the existence of suffering sentient beings there is no way to generate loving kindness and compassion, no way to actualize bodhicitta, no way to progress along the path. There's no way to actualize the Mahayana path, to complete it, to eliminate all the defilements and achieve all the qualities of cessation, to attain all realizations without depending on the kindness of sentient beings. No way.

Similarly, the Buddha showed the path to liberation, including the three higher trainings of morality, concentration and wisdom. When you achieve liberation from samsara by following that path, you do so by depending on the Buddha. However, without the existence of the obscured, suffering sentient beings, there is no way to accomplish the three higher trainings—no way to practice morality; no way to achieve shamatha, calm abiding, perfect concentration; and no way to attain great insight by realizing emptiness through analysis and then unifying it with shamatha, producing the extremely refined rapturous ecstasy through which that great insight is derived. Thus, without depending on the existence of sentient beings, you cannot actualize the path and attain liberation from samsara even for yourself.

Similarly, you cannot receive even good rebirths or happiness in future lives without depending on the existence of the suffering, obscured sentient beings. Why not? Because even though the Buddha has taught the practice of morality—the cause of happiness in future lives, including upper rebirths—without the base, the existence of suffering sentient beings, there's no way to practice it. It is on the basis of sentient beings that we make vows not to kill, steal, engage in sexual misconduct, lie and so forth. Sentient beings are the foundation of our vows not to give this harm or that. Without the existence of sentient beings, we cannot engage in these practices, the cause of happiness. Without the existence of sentient beings, we have no way to achieve any happiness whatsoever, no way to experience the slightest comfort in our daily lives, any enjoyment or sense pleasure up to the highest enlightenment. Every single happiness we ever experience comes to us through the kindness of sentient beings, depends upon them.

Since all happiness comes from virtue and the virtue we create is the holy action of the Buddha, we depend on the Buddha for whatever happiness we experience, achieve, receive. Similarly, all our happiness also depends on the kindness of sentient beings. That's why Shantideva asks why don't we respect sentient beings in the same way we respect the Buddha, why don't we treat sentient beings in the same way that we treat the Buddha. Whatever benefit, whatever realizations we derive from the Buddha, we derive the same complete benefit from all sentient beings, from each sentient being. The inconceivable benefits we get by making just one light offering, one water bowl offering or one hand prostration to a statue of the Buddha, whichever aspect is taken, we get the same benefits from sentient beings.

In the *Tune of Brahma Sutra Clarifying Karma*, Guru Shakyamuni Buddha mentions ten benefits of making extensive light offerings.[5] You also receive these ten important benefits the moment you put your palms together to a statue or painting of the Buddha, including achieving the path of the *arya* beings, the actual path that eradicates your gross delusions, or defilements, and through which you attain liberation from samsara. And then with bodhicitta you can eliminate also

---

[5] See *Teachings from the Vajrasattva Retreat*, page 625.

the subtle defilements and reach enlightenment. Even if the buddha to whom you press your palms together is merely visualized and there's no actual physical holy object such as a statue, painting or picture, you still derive these ten benefits. All this is through the kindness of sentient beings.

Even though the immediate source of these benefits of prostrating to the holy object is the buddha, when you trace the evolution back you will find that their actual source is sentient beings, that you received these ten benefits through the kindness of each sentient being. The root of all the temporary and ultimate happiness you get from holy objects— statues, stupas or paintings or pictures of buddha—is sentient beings. The inconceivable skies of benefit that you gain by circumambulating, prostrating, putting your palms together, or making offerings to these holy objects derives from sentient beings. Sentient beings are the root of all this happiness, all this good karma.

Rebirth in the lower realms

During each session of a Vajrasattva retreat we purify vast amounts of negative karma. First of all, think just how heavy one single complete negative karma is. For example, gossiping, ill will, stealing, sexual misconduct, killing and so forth. Leave aside the ripening aspect result, rebirth in the lower realms, such as the hell realms, or the hungry ghost realms, where the heaviest hunger and thirst are experienced for tens of thousands of years.

For us humans, it's not sufficient that we get enough food to fill our stomachs. We have to like it as well. It's not sufficient that the food we get fills our stomachs and is enough to live on. It should also be something we enjoy.

Compare the lives of us humans with those of the hungry ghosts, who can't find even a damp patch of ground let alone even a spoonful of water for hundreds of thousands of years. Pretas can't find a scrap of food for hundreds of thousands of years. Forget about their filling their stomachs every day, they can't even do it over a lifetime. Imagine what an incredible shock it would be for us if something happened and we had to go without food or water for a week; nothing to eat; nothing to drink. Of course, in the case of *nyung-nä*, it's different. It's only a day without food and drink and we know we're going to eat the next morning. But we'd find it terrible to have to experience this not under nyung-nä conditions. If our food and drink stopped for a day for reasons other than Dharma practice, we'd freak out. Our bodies would freak out, our minds would freak out. Everything would freak out... even our houses would freak out! Anyway, I'm comparing us to hungry ghosts because I myself am quite fussy about food. However, the hungry ghosts have unbearably heavy sufferings like that.

So, as I often mention, as it says in the teachings, the heat of the fire when the world comes to an end is sixty or seventy times greater than that of all the fires of our human world put together, but one tiny spark from the hell realm is seven times hotter than that. When the world ends, there's all this wind and fire that destroy everything. For example, when a volcano erupts and lava, that liquid fire, pours out, it melts everything in its path; even the rocks it touches melt. Normally, humans' fire cannot melt rocks, but lava does. So the end of the world fire is like that—everything, even huge rocky mountains, gets burned.

So, one tiny spark in the hell realm is seven times hotter than the world-ending fire.

Similarly, the energy of the cold hells is beyond compare with anything we know. The combined energy of the ice and cold of our world is great pleasure compared to that of the cold hells.

Also, even when you discover one new wrinkle on your body, you get so shocked; your mind is terrified. One more gray hair; one more wrinkle. It's such a shock. Therefore, there's no question that after having had this human body you couldn't stand reincarnating as an animal. Having been born human, it would be unbearable to see your consciousness migrate into an animal body. For example, how would you feel if your body gradually turned into that of a cat? Starting with your face; slowly your face becoming that of a cat. Even though you keep many cats around, you like cats, could you bear it? Not your whole body—just your head. Or perhaps starting from the tail? Or your body gradually turning into that of a snake? You couldn't stand it. But it's exactly the same—your consciousness leaves this body and migrates into the next. It's the same mental continuum, the same continuity of mind. It's your mind that migrates into the body of a snake, cockroach, mouse or cat. Exactly the same consciousness, the same mind; the one you have now.

So if you can't stand discovering one more wrinkle, one gray hair, your mind gets so freaked out, how will you be able to bear being reborn into an animal body, your body becoming that of an animal? There's no way. Even as a human being, *while* you are a human being, not having an animal body, if something changes, something decays, you can't stand it. You need so many instruments to repair the damage, so many chemicals to color it, so much effort and expense to reshape, uplift and so forth.

Imagine that you're born a cat or a dog, eating the same food, drinking the same water every day from that same container, the same thing from the same shop day after day. Even if you visualize yourself like that, a pet living with people, compared to other animals, those who live in the wild, you're actually very rich, very well-off. But even that you can't stand, can't bear.

Other suffering results

To conclude what I'm saying, the ripening aspect result of one single complete negative karma is rebirth in the lower realms, such as I've just been describing. However, there are three other types of suffering result, which we experience later, when we're finally, once again, born human. One is the possessed result, the unhealthy or fearful environment into which you're born. Even though you're born human, you find yourself in a place that endangers your life, that is filthy, dirty, full of excrement and garbage, where people cheat each other, where resources are scarce, there's no food or other means of living, where there's constant drought, nothing grows, there's much fighting, many wars—dreadful places like that.

Then there's the result similar to the cause where what you did to others in the past, the harm you gave them, comes back to harm you in return. Even though you are born human, you receive harm similar to that which you inflicted upon others in the past.

And finally, there's the result similar to the cause, where you engage in the same negative actions again. You create the same negative karma—gossiping, killing, sexual misconduct, ill will, slander and so forth—over and over again. No matter how much trouble you get into by doing these things, getting punished, imprisoned, fined or penalized, you can't stop yourself from creating these negative actions. Even though you think they're bad and that you should stop, you find it difficult to do so; your mind is very uncontrolled.

So again, you create the same negative karma in that life, and that again brings the four suffering results, one of which is creating that same negative karma yet again. That complete action, too, has the four suffering results, including that of doing it again, and so it goes, on and on, like that. If you don't purify a negative karma created today—such as gossiping, ill will, sexual misconduct and so forth—it will go on and on, and you will keep creating the result similar to the cause, bringing the four suffering results. One of these is again creating the result similar to the cause, which itself brings the four suffering results, and in this way your samsara becomes endless. There's no end to your suffering, no end at all. Your suffering becomes endless.

Here we're talking about just one negative karma done today. We're not talking about all of today's negative karma, yesterday's negative karma, this year's negative karma, this life's negative karma, previous lives' negative karma. We're not talking about all that. We're just talking about one negative karma done today, such as gossiping or sexual misconduct; just one negative karma. If it is not purified it makes suffering endless; the suffering goes on and on.

Therefore, by doing Vajrasattva practice or even the Thirty-five Buddhas just once—not taking into account all the other different practices but simply considering doing Vajrasattva meditation or reciting the powerful names of the Thirty-five Buddhas just once—you can purify not only having to experience rebirth in the lower realms but also the worst of the four results—that really bad one, the terrifying one, the one that is the worst of all, worse even than rebirth in hell—the result of engaging in the same negative actions again and again. These practices have the power to purify that.

Of the three suffering results that you experience in the human realm, that of creating the same negative karma over and over again is the worst because it makes your suffering endless. It is more terrifying than rebirth in hell because once you have experienced one rebirth in hell, it's over; that karma has finished. Hell suffering is not endless. You don't experience it continuously. When that hell karma finishes, the suffering of hell stops; the vision, the karmic appearance of hell, ceases.

Much more terrifying than that is the result similar to the cause where you engage in the same negative karma over and over again. That is the most terrifying of the four karmic results because it ensures that without end, you will be reborn again and again in the lower realms, as well as later having to experience all the other sufferings of the human realm. Therefore, the bad habit is worse than the suffering of hell. Putting it another way, it's like that.

The four remedial powers

What I'm saying here is that by doing the practice of confession with the four remedial powers [nyen-po tob-zhi], you can stop each of the four suffering results. By practicing the power of dependence [ten gyi tob], you purify the possessed result, finding yourself in a suffering environment. Here, by taking refuge, depending on Buddha, Dharma and Sangha, you purify the negative karma you have created with those holy objects. By generating bodhicitta, depending on sentient beings, you purify the negative karma you have created with them.

Then, the power of feeling regret for the negative actions [*nam-pa sünjin-pa'i tob*] purifies the result similar to the cause in experience.

The power that I translate as "the remedy of always enjoying," which in Tibetan is *nyen-po kun-tu chö-pa'i tob*—I think the meaning might be that by purifying negative karma, you get to enjoy happiness all the time, but I'm not completely sure—this is the remedy to the ripening aspect result, rebirth in the lower realms.

Finally, the power of determining not to commit those negative actions again [*nye-pa lä-lar dog-pa'i tob*] is the remedy for the suffering result similar to the cause where you continuously create those negative karmas again and again, which, as I explained, is much more terrifying, much worse than the suffering of hell itself.

The reason I'm going into all this in detail is so that you can understand, feel the kindness of sentient beings and therefore cherish them more than you do.

Through just one practice—reciting the Thirty-five Buddhas' names or doing the Vajrasattva meditation with the four remedial powers—you can avoid having to experience incredible unbearable suffering; you can purify so much negative karma. For example, one of today's negative karmas, such as gossiping—through these practices you can either stop its four suffering results from arising altogether, or if you can't stop them completely, at least you can lighten or shorten their effect. Instead of having to undergo hundreds of thousands of lifetimes of inconceivable suffering for eons in the lower realms, perhaps you can experience the result in this life as some kind of trouble, such as illness or *lung* [wind disease].

It's a strange thing about *lung*. I don't think I've ever heard Theravadins talk about it, but as soon as you encounter Tibetan Buddhism, you come to know about *lung*. First, you're introduced to Tibetan Buddhism, second, to *lung*—that very famous *lung*! I'm also not sure that Zen practitioners talk about *lung*; so far I haven't heard them do so. Anyway, after doing those purifying practices, instead of causing you to experience eons of suffering in the lower realms, your negative karma can manifest in this life as *lung*.

Frequently, Dharma practitioners who live their lives with a good heart, dedicated to others—or even those who haven't met Buddhism but have good hearts, strong compassion and loving kindness and dedicate their lives to others—purify much negative karma. Through their dedicated attitude and the service they offer others, they purify so much.

Sometimes you will find that meditators who practice strongly, who lead pure lives of renunciation, experience many sicknesses and problems, one after another. Of course, whether these experiences become a problem to them or not depends on how they think. Something that appears as a problem to others might not be a problem for them. It depends on how they look at the situation. Cancer or other serious illnesses can be taken as a very positive sign, because it means that the person will not have to experience many hundreds of thousands of lifetimes of heavy suffering results in the lower realms for incredible lengths of time from just one negative karma. That karma manifests as an illness in this life and finishes in that way. In such cases, it's a very positive, very good thing that happened.

Such heavy karmas can also finish simply by manifesting as other people criticizing you. The teachings talk about this as being one of the benefits of bodhicitta. Due to the power of bodhicitta, the good heart, instead of having to experience heavy suffering in either the human realm or the lower realms for incredible lengths of time, certain heavy negative karmas can get purified by manifesting as people criticizing or blaming you in this life. They finish as simply as that. Or they manifest as other experiences in this life such as migraine headaches, toothaches, nightmares, fearful dreams—things like that can finish heavy negative karmas that would otherwise have to be experienced as unbearable sufferings for great lengths of time.

Therefore, the teachings advise us that when problems like this arise, we should see them as positive and recognize them as signs of the power of our practice—that they are the manifestations of negative karma that is finishing much more lightly than it could have—and see them as positive.

Even if by practicing the remedy of vowing not to commit negative actions again—the antidote to the result similar to the cause of creating the same negative karmas again and again—with Vajrasattva or the Thirty-five Buddhas, you could avoid having to experience the four suffering results of just one negative karma, that would still be incredible peace. You would stop the constant suffering that arises from continuously creating the result similar to the cause, which brings suffering without end. You wouldn't have to go through it again. The absence of that karma and suffering is peace—peace forever. By purifying these negative karmas you stop having to experience the suffering result that happens again and again. So the everlasting peace and happiness that you experience in all your future lives from purifying these negative karmas comes from Vajrasattva or the Thirty-five Buddhas.

Purification comes from sentient beings

How does it come about that Vajrasattva's mantra has such power; that reciting even the names of the Thirty-five Buddhas has such power? It happens due to sentient beings. Just as crops come from a field, these purifying abilities come from sentient beings. The Thirty-five Buddhas became enlightened by depending on sentient beings. How did they become enlightened? By depending on sentient beings. Similarly, Vajrasattva came about because of sentient beings, through the existence of suffering sentient beings.

So far I've been talking about just one negative karma, but by practicing Vajrasattva or the Thirty-five Buddhas, by reciting their names and doing prostrations, we can purify all the countless negative karmas created today, this week, this month, this year, this life; with Vajrasattva or the Thirty-five Buddhas we can purify all our past lives' negative karmas.

To get an appreciation for this, first we should understand how terrifying all the results of just one negative karma are. How much suffering it brings from life to life, and how unbelievable it is to be able to purify all that with Vajrasattva or the Thirty-five Buddhas; how much unbelievable peace and happiness it brings. We should also understand what an emergency it is that we purify all this; that we should purify it without even a second's delay. Whether the negative karma be gossiping or ill will or sexual misconduct or telling lies or whatever, it is urgent to purify it without delaying even a moment. That's just one, but through these practices we can purify all the negative karma we have created not only in this life but in all previous lives as well.

That we have the opportunity to do all this purification with Vajrasattva or the Thirty-five Buddhas is due to the kindness of all sentient beings—those around us now, at home or wherever we are, and all the rest of the sentient beings. Vajrasattva and the Thirty-five Buddhas became enlightened through the kindness of each sentient being. That's one thing. That's how each of us has received this opportunity to purify ourselves.

Lama Atisha explained that the Thirty-five Buddhas' names are so powerful because in the past, when they were bodhisattvas, they made many dedication prayers to be able to benefit sentient beings by purifying their negative karma. One of them made specific dedications to be able to purify this kind of negative karma, another made specific dedications to be able to purify that kind of negative karma, and so forth. As bodhisattvas, they made many prayers to be able to benefit sentient beings, including us, who are reciting the Thirty-five Buddhas' names right now. They made prayers that when they became buddhas, sentient beings would be able to purify those various specific negative karmas by reciting their names.

A buddha has many good qualities, such as the ten powers, one of which is the power of prayer. So because a buddha has achieved the power of prayer, whatever prayers were made in the past are actualized. Therefore, when we recite the Thirty-five Buddhas' names, they have the power to purify all those negative karmas. How does it happen that these Buddhas' names have all that power, that by reciting their names we can purify so much negative karma? Because originally they made many prayers with bodhicitta and generated the great intention to benefit sentient beings in this way. That will, that intention, has power. Then, when they became buddhas, they achieved the quality of possessing the ten powers, one of which is the power of prayer, and that's what gives power to their names. Now, when we recite their names, it affects our minds. That's how it works. The reason their names have so much power is because it came from their bodhicitta.

However, their bodhicitta was generated in dependence upon sentient beings—each and every sentient being. Therefore, by reciting each buddha's name, we can purify all these different negative karmas that we always engage in; the negative karma that we create in this life and have created in our previous lives. That we can purify as much as we want, that we have the opportunity to do this, is basically due to sentient beings, the kindness of each sentient being. So like that, the evolution goes down to the root, sentient beings. It comes from there.

As I've mentioned before, if you generate compassion for one sentient being, whether it's an insect or a human, you achieve enlightenment from that sentient being. The stronger the compassion for that sentient being you can generate, the quicker you reach enlightenment. No matter how much Highest Yoga Tantra you practice, how much you meditate on the generation stage, the completion stage, if you don't have compassion, if you don't generate compassion for that sentient being, that insect or that human, you cannot attain enlightenment. And the stronger your compassion, the quicker you get enlightened. That's why sentient beings are so precious—because you can derive so much from them. Each sentient being is extremely precious to your life.

All the good qualities of Sangha—those of the bodhisattvas, such as the six paramitas, bodhicitta; those of the arhats, their psychic powers;

the realizations of the dakas and dakinis, the wisdom of non-dual bliss and voidness; the qualities of the Dharma protectors, their ability to accomplish the four actions and so forth—all this is a result of the kindness of sentient beings. All this is achieved by depending on the kindness of sentient beings.

All the good qualities of Dharma—all the benefits of renunciation, bodhicitta, emptiness, the ten bhumis, the five paths, the qualities of the path, from guru devotion up to the goal, enlightenment—derive from sentient beings, depend on the kindness of sentient beings.

And all the good qualities of Buddha—the state of omniscient mind, complete compassion, perfect power, the skies of good qualities of the Buddha's holy body, speech and mind—are achieved in dependence upon the kindness of sentient beings. It comes from sentient beings; every single sentient being; by depending on the kindness of each and every one.

The power of compassion

For example, a story about one of the Vajrayogini lineage lamas, the monk Getsul Tsimbulwa, illustrates the power of compassion. In West Bengal there's a place called Odi. It's near Buxa, where the refugee monks from Sera, Ganden and Drepung monasteries who wanted to continue their studies lived for eight or nine years after fleeing Tibet. I lived there for about eight years. Not continuously, but on and off. There's a season that people from Bombay go to Odi on pilgrimage; thousands of them. There are many caves in the rocky mountains there and it can be quite dangerous; you have to hold on to chains as you walk along. You hear sounds or experience other signs, depending on how pure your mind is.

So, Getsul Tsimbulwa's guru, the great yogi Ngagpa Chöpawa, who was a layman, was on his way to Odi to practice the final stage of tantra that you do just before you get enlightened. It is called "entering the deeds of tantra," where I think that from ordinary people's point of view you appear to be crazy. You're not crazy but you look crazy. So you do that practice—entering the deeds of tantra—before becoming enlightened. He came to a river, and on the bank was a woman whose whole body was covered with leprosy sores, with pus oozing out everywhere. She asked him to carry her on his back to the other side of the river, but he ignored her and went on his way.

A bit later, his disciple Getsul Tsimbulwa came by, and as soon as he saw this poor woman—ravaged by leprosy, covered in sores, pus everywhere; something that most people would be too scared to go near, let alone touch—he felt unbearable compassion for her, and without any thought of how dirty she was, immediately picked her up, put her on his back and started across the river. However, when he reached the middle of the river, suddenly he saw her as the female deity Dorje Pagmo, Vajrayogini, who then took him to her pure land in his ordinary body, without his first having to die.

If you are born in the Vajrayogini pure land, it is definite, one hundred percent certain, that you will become enlightened in that lifetime. If you don't get enlightened as a human, the quickest way to do so is to go to a pure land such as that of Heruka or Vajrayogini. So, she wasn't an ordinary being, but because of his impure karma, Getsul Tsimbulwa saw her as an ordinary sentient being; sick, covered in leprosy sores.

Nevertheless, filled with unbearable compassion, with no thought of dirtiness, he sacrificed his life to carry her across the river, and during that short time, his negative, impure karma was completely purified. Because of that compassion and his sacrificing his life for that living being, in the short time it took him to carry her half-way across the river, the negative karma that projected her in an ordinary appearance instead of in her true nature as Vajrayogini, that blocked him from seeing her as an enlightened being, was completely purified.

Therefore, in the middle of the river, because of his unbearable compassion for her, the negative karma that projected the impure view was purified. Since there was no longer any impure view, the impure appearance of a sick woman disappeared and he was able to go to Vajrayogini's pure land and get enlightened there. The teacher, Ngagpa Chöpawa, the yogi, didn't do that, but his disciple did.

That shows how precious sentient beings are, in that you can derive infinite benefit from them and achieve every single happiness, and the stronger the compassion you can generate, the quicker you gain realizations and attain enlightenment.

Similarly, even though Maitreya Buddha generated bodhicitta much earlier than Guru Shakyamuni Buddha did, because Guru Shakyamuni Buddha's compassion and bodhicitta were stronger, Guru Shakyamuni Buddha became enlightened before Maitreya Buddha. How this happened was that in a previous life they were brothers and one day they were passing through Namo Buddha, in Nepal, when they came across a family of tigers, a mother and her four cubs, who were starving to death. They continued on their journey home, but because of the unbearable compassion Guru Shakyamuni Buddha felt for the tigers, he came back later and sacrificed his body so that they could live. He and Maitreya Buddha were both bodhisattvas at the time, and Maitreya Buddha also felt compassion, but didn't give up his life for the tigers. But because his bodhicitta was stronger, Guru Shakyamuni Buddha did, and as a result he became enlightened before Maitreya Buddha.

Therefore, it seems that in our lives, of all the billions of different Dharma practices that we could do, of all the many different forms of practice that there are, the most important is that of compassion for sentient beings.

The best thing in life

As I said at the beginning of this talk, the best thing you can do with your life is to cherish sentient beings. Every day, whatever your circumstances, whether you are happy or unhappy, up or down, any time anywhere, cherish sentient beings. It can happen that when you are unhappy, you give sentient beings up, and only when you are happy do you think of others. Well, it can also happen that when you are happy you give them up too, but anyway, no matter whether you're happy or unhappy, whatever circumstances you find yourself in, keep as your only goal in life the welfare of sentient beings. Continuously, every day, all the time, always think how precious they are, how they are most precious. Even Buddha, Dharma and Sangha come from sentient beings— the Thirty-five Buddhas, Vajrasattva. Therefore, sentient beings are the most precious thing in your life.

If you live your life with this attitude, even if you don't do three year retreats or study Dharma extensively, you will have happiness now and in the future. With this attitude, your future will always be good, the best. Living your life with this attitude, think that every sentient being, every person, you meet is most precious—at home, at work, at your Dharma center, feel that every person you see is the most precious one in your life. In this way you will not only experience happiness now but will also experience the best possible future, and at the time of death will feel no regrets—only happiness and joy. Even though your life might have started with suffering, it will end with joy.

With the thought of cherishing others, serving them comes naturally, without difficulty. You will serve others happily, voluntarily, enjoyably. With this thought, serving others will become the best, most enjoyable thing you can do in your life. In that way, even though you might be doing exactly the same things that you were doing before, even though your job or your actions haven't changed, because your attitude is different, everything you do brings you happiness, fulfillment and joy.

Before, when you did things with ego, self-centered mind, you didn't enjoy life and encountered many problems. The same job, the same work—in a meditation center or in a city office—but there were always problems with other people, dissatisfaction with your work, a lot of unhappiness. But now, with this change of attitude, thinking that everyone is the most precious thing in your life, serving them comes naturally—not as a burden but as a joy. Serving others becomes enjoyment, not a job. You are giving something to others, so you feel happiness, satisfaction, fulfillment and joy.

Lama Zopa Rinpoche gave this teaching 27 February 1999.

3

The Purpose of Being Human

A s I MENTIONED BEFORE, you should know the meaning of your life, the reason you are alive, the purpose of having taken this precious human body at this time, especially this perfect human rebirth, which has eight freedoms and ten richnesses—you should know this, not just intellectually but deeply, so that you transform your attitude accordingly and live your life in harmony with that purpose. What is the purpose of your life? It is to live for the benefit of others.

Therefore, compassion is the most important meditation, or practice, you can do. Even though the Buddha's teachings talk about billions of different meditations, or practices, that you could spend your whole life doing, this is the most important—benefiting others; living your life with an attitude of compassion for others. This is the real purpose of life, the real meaning of your life.

If even you have only an hour to live, a minute to live, the purpose of life is still to live for the benefit of others, with a good heart, with compassion for others. Even if you have only a minute to live, only a minute of this precious human body left, the most important thing you can practice is compassion; nothing else.

The same thing would be true were you to have a hundred years to live, a thousand years to live, even an eon to live. To fulfill your life's purpose, you would still have to live with compassion for others, for the benefit of others.

If you are enjoying a happy life, experiencing pleasure, in order for your life not to be empty, to be beneficial, useful, for others, you should practice compassion, live your life for the benefit of others.

If your life is unhappy, if you are experiencing relationship problems, if you have cancer or AIDS, if you are depressed, if your life is uncomfortable, even if you are encountering so many hundreds and hundreds of problems—health, relationship, job-related problems—that it seems as if you are drowning in a quagmire of problems, you should also practice compassion for others. If you can practice compassion at times like this, you will still be making your life meaningful, beneficial for others, useful for others, and therefore—by benefiting others—you will be constantly making your life beneficial for yourself. Cherishing others is the best way of cherishing yourself.

Cherishing others brings enlightenment

Cherishing others means that you don't harm others, and not harming others is not harming yourself. Even in terms of protection, this is the best way to protect your life. Similarly, when you cause others to be happy, you bring happiness to yourself. The karma created by making others happy causes you to experience happiness too; that's the kind of karma that results in happiness. Even if you don't want happiness, once you have created its cause, that's what results.

If you plant a seed in the ground and all the right conditions are present, such as perfect soil, water, and heat—everything is together and there are no obstacles—then no matter how much you pray for the plant not to grow, it will grow. It will definitely grow because the seed planted in the ground has met all the conditions necessary for growth; the cause and conditions have met. Since it is a dependent arising, it is inevitable that that flower or fruit will grow, no matter how much you pray for it not to.

Similarly, if you lead your everyday life with compassion, bringing as much happiness to others as you possibly can, the natural result will be for you yourself to experience happiness, both now and in the future—there's the immediate effect of peace of mind in this life and the long-term effect of happiness in all your future lives. All this is the definite result of bringing happiness and benefit to others.

Therefore, there is much to be gained by cherishing others, taking care of other living beings as you do yourself. Whether they are insects or humans, they are living beings just like you—wanting happiness; not wanting suffering. Just as you need the help of others to eliminate problems, so do they. Just as your happiness depends on others, so does theirs. Not only humans but also insects need your help. Their freedom from problems depends on you; their happiness depends on you.

Why is cherishing others, taking care of others as you do yourself, not harming but benefiting them, the best way of looking after yourself, taking care of yourself? Because it is through having a good heart, cherishing others, benefiting others, that all your own wishes get fulfilled.

In general, in the world, when others see a person who has a compassionate, loving nature, who is good-hearted, they get good vibrations, a positive feeling from that person. Even when strangers meet that person on the road, in airplanes, in offices or shops, just the sight of that person makes them happy, smile, want to chat. Because of your good heart, good vibrations, positive feeling, you make others happy. Even their facial expressions change to reflect their happy minds. Even if you aren't experiencing any problems, others keep offering you help.

When you have a good heart towards others, all your wishes for your own happiness get fulfilled by the way. Even though your motivation, like that of a bodhisattva, is only the happiness of others and you have not a single expectation of happiness for yourself, even if everything you do, twenty-four hours a day, is exclusively dedicated to the happiness of others with not a thought for your own, you yourself will experience all happiness.

Because of their realization of bodhicitta, the attitude of those holy beings, the bodhisattvas, is such that they totally renounce themselves for others; they have no thought for their own happiness but instead spend every moment seeking the happiness of others. So what happens? With bodhicitta, they are able to develop the ultimate wisdom realizing the very nature of the I—the self and the aggregates, the association of body and mind that is the base that is labeled I—and all other phenomena. Because of their bodhicitta and the ultimate wisdom they develop, they are able to eradicate all errors of mind, the cause of all suffering—both the gross defilements, the delusions of ignorance, attachment and aversion, and the subtle defilements, which are in the nature of imprints left on the mental continuum by the delusions.

This, then, is the special feature of bodhicitta, because with its support you can develop not only the wisdom realizing emptiness but can also stop the subtle defilements and thus become fully awakened, attaining the state of omniscience, the fully enlightened mind, knowing directly and without a single mistake, not only the gross karma but also every single subtle karma of each of the numberless sentient beings; seeing all their different characteristics, wishes and levels of intelligence; knowing every single method that suits the minds of all these different sentient beings at different times; and revealing the appropriate method that suits the mind of each individual sentient being at different times in order to guide that being from happiness to happiness, all the way up to enlightenment.

Thus, bodhicitta allows your wisdom to function such that it can overcome even the subtle defilements, making your mind fully enlightened. In this way, bodhicitta allows you to become a fully qualified guide, a perfectly enlightened being, and therefore to liberate numberless other sentient beings from samsara, the ocean of suffering, and bring them into the peerless happiness of full enlightenment.

So from where does this achievement of all those infinite enlightened qualities arise? Even the bodhisattvas on the ten levels [Skt: *bhumis*] have incredible, inconceivable qualities. Just a first level bodhisattva is able to meditate in hundreds of different concentrations, go to hundreds of different pure lands, reveal hundreds of different teachings to sentient beings. I don't recall exactly, but there are about eleven different things of which they can do hundreds. Then a second level bodhisattva can do a thousand different concentrations, go to a thousand pure lands, reveal a thousand different teachings to sentient beings, and so forth. Like this, as they progress higher and higher through the levels, they achieve more and more inconceivable qualities with which they can benefit other sentient beings. The bodhisattvas on the ninth and tenth levels possess inconceivable numbers of such qualities.

All these incredible qualities of the bodhisattva path, all the infinite qualities of the buddha's holy body, holy speech and holy mind, come from the root, renunciation of ego and the thought that seeks the happiness of oneself alone, and generation of the good heart, the thought that seeks the happiness of only other sentient beings. All those qualities come from this. All the infinite good qualities of Buddha, Dharma, the bodhisattvas' path, and Sangha, those arya and even ordinary bodhisattvas, come from the incredibly precious thought, the wish-fulfilling bodhicitta—renunciation of ego and self-centered mind and development of cherishing only others. They all come from this.

Those who can do this realize the best possible achievement. They renounce the self, they renounce the I, but they gain the best achievement, the greatest success. Not only do they find liberation forever from the cycle of death and rebirth and all the problems it brings, such as rebirth, old age, sickness, emotional problems and all other difficulties of life we experience, but they also attain everlasting liberation, everlasting freedom, everlasting happiness for themselves, and are able to bring skies of happiness to numberless other sentient beings. All this comes from the root, bodhicitta, that most precious holy mind, renouncing I, cherishing others.

Cherishing others overcomes suffering

We can understand how this is true from reading texts that tell the stories of Buddha's previous lives and the lives of other bodhisattvas, but we can also understand how a good heart is wish-fulfilling for your happiness from simple examples from the ordinary lives of common people in the world—how those whose minds are more compassionate in nature, who are good hearted, have much easier lives.

For example, if you are experiencing serious health problems, like cancer and so forth, but you have a good heart, your mind will be happy and peaceful because your main concern is not for yourself but for others; your concern is for other sentient beings. Therefore, your mind is peaceful. Even if you are dying, your mind is not disturbed because your concern is for others, not yourself. Even at the end of your life, at the very end of your human life, your experience of death is a happy one because your attitude is one of concern for others, not for I, not the self-cherishing, self-centered mind.

Even though things don't work out for you, you encounter many obstacles, your life is going wrong, none of this bothers you, your mind is undisturbed, always happy and peaceful, because the first priority in your life is the happiness of others. What concerns you most is others, not yourself. That's your goal. This attitude brings so much peace and happiness into your daily life, gives you so much satisfaction. Even if other people are causing you problems, hassling you, it doesn't bother your mind; your mind remains peaceful and happy.

In particular, with a good heart, compassion for others, whenever a problem arises, you experience it for others, on behalf of other sentient beings. If you experience happiness, you experience it for others. If you enjoy a luxury life, comfort, you dedicate it to others. And if you experience a problem, you experience it for others—for others to be free of problems and to have all happiness up to enlightenment, complete perfect peace and bliss. Wishing others to have all happiness, you experience problems on their behalf.

That gives you incredible satisfaction and fulfillment, but not only that. If you have that attitude, no matter how many problems you experience, when you encounter each one you feel like you have discovered a precious treasure. You see it as an incredible opportunity to dedicate yourself to others; a great chance to experience the sufferings of others, like bodhisattvas do, like Buddha did, like Jesus Christ did; to take upon yourself the suffering of others.

Even though others might find that problem unbearable, for you, who has this attitude, it's not a big bother, you don't find it particularly difficult, you're pretty easy about it—because of your good heart, that pure attitude of life. This makes your entire life very easy, very happy. Your heart is not hollow, not empty, but overflowing with fulfillment, brimming with joy. In this way, even should you encounter many problems, you live your life with joy. You enjoy your problems; you even enjoy your death.

No matter what happens, you enjoy it with bodhicitta, the thought that cherishes others. What ordinary people might find undesirable, the person with the good heart, the attitude of cherishing others, finds desirable because that person can make problems beneficial for other sentient beings. The person with a good heart, a compassionate mind, the thought of cherishing others, the bodhicitta attitude, makes the problem useful, beneficial for others. In this way, this person's experience of problems becomes a cause for the happiness of all sentient beings—not just temporary happiness but that of the highest, full enlightenment. Bodhicitta makes the person's experience of problems a cause for the happiness of all living beings. How? By transforming problems into the path to enlightenment.

Gen Jampa Wangdu

I often tell stories about Gen Jampa Wangdu, who was one of the most senior Tibetan meditators in India and meditated around Dharamsala and Dalhousie, guided by the ascetic lama, Dewo Gyüpe Rinpoche. After completing all his philosophical sutra studies and then completing the study of tantra, passing all his examinations and becoming a *lharampa* geshe, a geshe of the highest rank, Gen Jampa Wangdu went into solitude up in the mountains to actualize the path that he had been studying in the monastery from the time of his youth for so many years. He was a highly attained yogi and bodhisattva who had accomplished the highest tantra path, which has five stages—isolation of body, isolation of speech, isolation of mind, clear light and illusory body, and unification. So he had reached the highest levels of tantra and attained the illusory body.

In 1982, after the FPMT's first Dharma Celebration,[6] many of our sangha members took teachings from him on how to do the "pill" retreat—"Taking the Essence" [*chu-len*], a method of being able to retreat in very isolated places, far from everything, where food and drink are hard to find.[7] Instead of living on ordinary food, you live on special blessed pills, which gives you more time for your meditation practice and makes your mind clear and is an easy way to achieve the perfect concentration of calm abiding [Skt: *shamatha*; Tib: *shiné*]. Gen Jampa Wangdu was one of my gurus and I took the lineage of the chu-len teaching from him.

[6] Or, as it was called at the time, the Enlightened Experience Celebration.
[7] See http://www.lamayeshe.com/lamayeshe/tte.shtml

Once I was in Dharamsala, staying at Geshe Rabten Rinpoche's house, which was below the house of His Holiness Ling Rinpoche, the senior tutor of His Holiness the Dalai Lama. Geshe Rabten Rinpoche was my first teacher of philosophical texts, the debating text, *du-ra*; he was the one who started me off on those. These lamas' houses were near our center, Tushita. One night Gen Jampa Wangdu came back late after teachings and found that his house had been burgled. Of course, there was hardly anything worth stealing, but he found that the thief had taken his clock. That was it! But he was so happy that the thief had gotten himself a clock; he was so happy!

Serkong Dorje Chang

There's a similar story about the Serkong Dorje Chang, who lived in Nepal—the incarnation of the Serkong Dorje Chang who lived in Tibet at the beginning of the twentieth century and was also a lharampa geshe. A lharampa geshe is like the most highly qualified professor, a great scholar, but in this case not merely a scholar of words but also in experience of the path. Later he became one of the few lamas to be officially recognized by His Holiness the Thirteenth Dalai Lama to have attained high enough levels of the tantric path to be allowed to practice with a wisdom mother consort. The incarnation who lived in Nepal passed away some years ago and has been reborn and is now studying at Ganden Monastery in south India.

Normally my mind is full of doubt and superstition, but every time I would go to see him I would have no doubt that when I was in his presence, I was in the presence of Yamantaka. Not a single hesitation that

Serkong Dorje Chang was Yamantaka, an enlightened being, the most wrathful aspect of Manjushri, the buddha of wisdom. I was always one hundred percent certain that he was Yamantaka.

Serkong Dorje Chang was exactly the same as those ancient Indian yogis like Tilopa and Naropa, the forerunners of the lineage continued by Marpa and Milarepa, but living in the present time. Actually, one day, he himself told a monk that he was the embodiment of Marpa. That would happen, sometimes. On a good day—I don't mean weather-wise—when the time was right, Rinpoche would say many interesting things. At the end of the monks' annual summer retreat, *yar-né*, as part of the traditional *vinaya* practice, the monks from his monastery would go for *gag-yé*, release from the retreat. Usually it would be a picnic, where Rinpoche would tell the monks many interesting stories.

Sometimes Rinpoche and some monks would go to do pujas at bene-factors' houses in Kathmandu. When it was over they would return to their monastery on Swayambhunath mountain, which tourists call the "monkey temple" because there are so many monkeys on it. One of his monks was from our college, Sera-je. He was an assistant *umdze*, assistant leader of prayers—usually there are a few other monks who support the chant leader; he was one of those. So one day when they were all walking back to the monastery, Serkong Dorje Chang said to this monk, "In reality, I'm actually Marpa."

Serkong Tsenshab Rinpoche, who lived in Dharamsala and was one of His Holiness the Dalai Lama's gurus—he gave His Holiness a commentary on Atisha's *Lamp on the Path to Enlightenment* and some other teachings as well—is also one of my gurus and has been exceptionally kind to me. Even though from my side I am very lazy and lacking in ability, from Rinpoche's side he would always teach me anything I asked for. He always looked after me, guided me and was really so very kind.

Serkong Tsenshab Rinpoche's father was the Serkong Dorje Chang who lived in Tibet—the one who after becoming a lharampa geshe attained the highest levels of tantra and practiced with a wisdom mother consort. Serkong Tsenshab Rinpoche was his son, and later, when Serkong Dorje Chang was reborn, Serkong Tsenshab Rinpoche became his teacher, the teacher of his father's incarnation. Serkong Dorje Chang also told the Sera-je monk that Serkong Tsenshab Rinpoche was Marpa's son, Tarma Dodé, and another incarnate lama, Tsechog Ling Rinpoche, was Milarepa. So Serkong Dorje Chang said, "In reality, we are like this."

His Holiness Serkong Tsenshab Rinpoche always used to say, "Oh, Serkong Dorje Chang—those ancient yogis were something like that." He wouldn't say many words, didn't tell any stories, but would just kind of label, like that. Once Serkong Dorje Chang was traveling to Bodh Gaya—perhaps on pilgrimage or for teachings from His Holiness the Dalai Lama—and his monks' robes, the required yellow ones, were left in a taxi in Patna. Later, when his attendant told Rinpoche that they had been lost, stolen, he said, "Oh, that's very good," meaning that he was happy that the thieves might get some use out of them, that it was worthwhile that they'd been stolen.

Even though I never received any initiations or oral transmissions of texts from beginning to end from Serkong Dorje Chang, I regard him as one of my gurus. Basically, that's what he is. When Lama Yeshe and I arrived in Nepal, we stayed outside Kathmandu at the Gelug monastery at Boudhanath, near the precious great stupa. It was the only Gelug monastery at Boudhanath and at that time might have been the only Tibetan monastery with monks. We stayed upstairs there for about a year.

Every year during the fourth Tibetan month, at Saka Dawa, they would do *nyung-nä*. The year we were there it was sponsored by a benefactor who had a connection with another lama from Swayambhunath, Drubtob Rinpoche, not Serkong Dorje Chang. According to his devotion, the benefactor wanted Drubtob Rinpoche to give the ordination of the eight Mahayana precepts. But the Gelug monks weren't so interested in him. They wanted Serkong Dorje Chang because Drubtob Rinpoche practiced the Most Secret Hayagriva deity that our Sera-je College practices and they didn't—they thought it was a Nyingma deity or something like that. So for this kind of reason there was some conflict.

The monks prevailed, and Serkong Dorje Chang was invited to give the ordination of the eight Mahayana precepts in the early morning. So Rinpoche came in carrying the precepts text, opened it, and said, "If your guru tells you to lick fresh, hot kaka, get down on the ground immediately and lick it!" Then with his tongue outstretched and making a slurping sound, he imitated a dog licking up excrement. "That's how to practice Dharma," he said. Then he left. That was the motivation he gave us before giving precepts. But he didn't actually give us precepts. He just gave that advice and left. It was like an atomic explosion—a very powerful teaching. It really moved the mind. Just on the basis of that instruction, I took him as a guru. That's all he taught that morning. But he's somebody who knows everything; a great yogi, as Serkong Tsenshab Rinpoche said.

Serkong Dorje Chang would often circumambulate the precious

stupa at Swayambhunath, the main, original holy object in Kathmandu. To people who didn't know who he was or the qualities he embodied, he would appear as a very simple monk. They'd think he knew nothing—a simple monk, mala in hand, circumambulating the stupa. That's how he appeared to ordinary people. He might have appeared like he knew nothing, but in reality, he knew everything.

Sometimes he'd be circumambulating with all the other people and if the time was right, if it was their lucky day, he'd suddenly turn to a complete stranger and say, "You don't have much longer to live," or "You're going to die in a month"; "Better do prostrations to the Thirty-five Buddhas." Something like that. Rinpoche would make predictions and advise the people what to do. But if the time wasn't right, if it was not the day of your good fortune, even if you asked him something directly, he would say, "Oh, I know nothing. I'm completely ignorant."

I first heard about Serkong Dorje Chang when I was in Buxa—stories about his suddenly disappearing and reappearing somewhere else and his attendants having to go look for him; many stories like that. Therefore, soon after we arrived in Nepal we went very anxiously to Swayambhunath to meet him. He was staying at a benefactor's house because he didn't have his own monastery at that time and had been kicked out of the monastery where he was staying due to some political problem. It was a Nepalese house and he was staying upstairs. When we arrived, this very simple monk came down the steps and we asked him, "Where's Serkong Dorje Chang?" He told us to wait and went back inside the house through another door, not the one he'd come out of. Then we went upstairs to Rinpoche's room and the simple monk we'd seen downstairs was sitting on the bed. It was Serkong Dorje Chang.

Our first Western disciple, who had already been ordained a nun, Princess Zina Rachevsky—she was descended from Russian nobility—was with us at the time. Serkong Dorje Chang had a big pile of texts next to his bed, so she just blurted out, "Please read us something from those." Normally you don't ask like that! In fact, usually when we took her to see high lamas we'd help her prepare the Dharma questions she was going to ask. Anyway, that's what she said, and Serkong Dorje Chang replied, "No, no, no. I know nothing, I know nothing." But then Rinpoche gave some unbelievably profound teachings.

I can't remember what they were! But they were unbelievably profound; really deep. All I can remember is the essence, which was, "If your guru is sitting there on the floor, you must think that it is Guru Shakyamuni Buddha who is sitting there." I can't remember the exact words, which were much more than that, but that was the essence of Rinpoche's advice to her.

One of Rinpoche's supporters was a Tibetan from Amdo. He was the monastery's biggest benefactor. Every year he would invite Rinpoche and his monks to his house to recite the *Praises to the Twenty-one Taras* 100,000 times and they would stay there for however many weeks it took to do that. Serkong Dorje Chang would be there for the duration. This major benefactor built all the monks' rooms at the monastery; something significant like that. One day he came to the monastery to see Rinpoche and Rinpoche said, "And who are you?" pretending not to know him. Then Rinpoche's attendant explained who he was, but Rinpoche still didn't show any signs of recognition. This man was a big businessman and used to sell buddha statues in order to support his family. He must have done something really negative just before coming to see Rinpoche, so perhaps as a sign of that obscuration, Rinpoche manifested the aspect of not knowing who he was. There's no way he could have forgotten him.

The monastery used to have this really big pot for making tea and food for all the monks. One day it was stolen, but when the monks told Rinpoche about it, he said, "Invite the thieves here and offer them a *khatag* to thank them for taking it." But I'm not sure that the monastery followed through on that!

Once the bodhisattva Togme Zangpo, author of *The Thirty-seven Practice of Bodhisattvas*, was invited to a monastery to give teachings or attend a puja and received many offerings. Soon after leaving the monastery he and his party were held up by robbers, who tied them up and stole all the offerings. I don't know if they beat them as well, but they certainly took everything. Before they could leave, the bodhisattva Togme Zangpo asked them to wait so that he could dedicate to them everything they had taken. Of course, they'd already taken everything physically, but he insisted on making prayers for their well-being. Then he advised them to avoid going near the monastery when they left, otherwise the monks would see that they'd stolen the offerings and would beat them up!

The healing power of compassion

The conclusion of all this is as I mentioned before. Compassion for other sentient beings is the best method, the best antidote for eliminating life obstacles; the best puja to eliminate obstacles to the success of both your Dharma practice—your gaining realizations—and your worldly work—such as your business affairs.

Once in Tibet there was a very wealthy family whose daughter was possessed by spirits. She'd gone completely wild and crazy. They invited many local lay lamas who normally did pujas and prayers for people in that area, but nothing helped. One day a simple monk came by begging for alms, so they invited him upstairs to see if he could do anything for their daughter. Maybe the monk was a geshe, I don't know, but anyway, he tried the tantric ritual of the *geg-tor*—giving a *torma* to the interferers, like when we offer those three tormas at the beginning of initiations. But when he recited the mantra NAMO SARVA TATHAGATA BEU MEGA ... SOHA and lifted up the torma, offering it to the interferers, she just imitated his actions and recited the same mantra back. So he realized that what he was doing wasn't helping!

Therefore he stopped performing the ritual and instead wrapped his *zen* [monk's upper robe] around his head and meditated on compassion—for the suffering of the spirit and the suffering of the girl. At that point the spirit spoke to him through the girl, saying, "Please let me go. I will leave her," and she was released. The girl who had been completely wild and crazy through spirit possession was finally freed by compassion. That was the only thing that could heal her. This is just one example of how compassion is one of the best, most powerful ways of eliminating obstacles.

The remedy of compassion is also the best medicine for healing sickness, the best antidote to disease. There are many stories of people who have recovered from illness by doing the compassionate practice of *tong-len*, where by taking others' suffering onto yourself you cure your own disease.

There was a Dharma student in Singapore who had AIDS. His first guru was Rato Rinpoche, a very high lama living in Dharamsala, who himself had taken the aspect of having Parkinson's disease. Through the lady who translates at the Tibetan Library for Geshe Sonam Rinchen [Ruth Sonam], Rinpoche dictated the tong-len practice for this student—taking other sentient beings suffering onto himself and giving his own happiness, merit, body and so forth to others—and had her send it to him in Singapore.

The student practiced tong-len for four days and then went to the hospital for a check-up, where they could find no trace of AIDS. When he told me about this I thought he must have done many hours of meditation during those four days, so I asked him how much he'd done. "Five minutes a day," he said. Five minutes a day!

So what happened? While he was meditating, he felt unbearable compassion for all the other people who were suffering from sickness, especially AIDS, and felt no concern whatsoever for his own problems. He felt unbelievable compassion; he could not bear the suffering of AIDS that others were experiencing. During those five minutes tears of compassion poured down his cheeks. So even though he practiced for only five minutes a day, he practiced very, very strongly. The compassion he generated was very strong, and that strong compassion for only five minutes a day for four days, that special bodhicitta practice of taking other sentient beings' suffering onto himself and giving them his own happiness and merit and so forth, was enough to overcome his AIDS.

How does compassion heal illness? How does it work? Sicknesses come from negative karma—non-virtuous actions, actions done with attachment, with an impure mind—and the most powerful purifier of such negative karma is compassion, bodhicitta—the altruistic mind cherishing others and seeking enlightenment.

As Shantideva said in the chapter on the benefits of bodhicitta in his *Guide to the Bodhisattva's Way of Life*—and I'll translate this a little loosely so that the meaning of the verse becomes clear—"By relying on a hero you can free yourself from great danger."[8]

This means that if, for example, you are going to be executed or there's some other danger to your life, sometimes the only way you can free yourself is by taking refuge in a very powerful person. The danger we face is the practically inexhaustible, powerful, negative karma, as heavy as a mountain, that we have created in this life and collected throughout our hundreds of thousands, in fact beginningless, previous lives. The hero who can save us from this is bodhicitta, the practice of which can purify these mountains of powerful, heavy negative karma in a moment. By relying on the heroic mind of bodhicitta—the attitude that renounces the I and cherishes others—we can purify all this heavy negative karma in the time it takes to snap our fingers.

Shantideva continues, "So, why don't conscientious beings rely on this?"

In other words, he's saying, if you're a careful person, why don't you practice bodhicitta? Bodhicitta has such incredible purifying power; if you're intelligent, careful, conscientious and mindful, why don't you practice bodhicitta? Compassion is such a powerful, positive mind that when the man from Singapore generated it so strongly, he purified so much negative karma that he purified the karma that caused him to

[8] Chapter 1, verse 13

have AIDS. Because compassion purifies negative karma, after four days he was free of AIDS. That's just one example.

Therefore, compassion is not only the best puja, like in the story of the girl possessed by a spirit, not only the best method of eliminating life obstacles, but also the best, sublime medicine for healing sickness. What is the best way of overcoming cancer and all other illnesses through meditation, with your own mind? It is by developing compassion, by generating compassion for the suffering of others.

Whenever you experience pain in your eye or anywhere else, as soon as it starts, the immediate cure is the practice of the special bodhicitta meditation, taking other sentient beings' suffering on yourself and giving them all your happiness, merit, body and possessions. With compassion take their suffering on yourself and with loving kindness give your happiness, merit, body, possessions and so forth to others. As soon as the pain starts, however painful it is, the immediate cure, the immediate antidote, the best, most powerful method of dealing with it is tonglen, taking and giving, the special practice of bodhicitta. Even though normally I am very lazy about practicing Dharma, through the kindness of pain I reminded to practice.

This meditation is so powerful that even before you start the actual practice, the moment you start preparing your mind to take on the suffering of others, the pain stops. This shows that even the slightest thought of exchanging yourself for others, just thinking of taking on the suffering of others, just preparing your mind to do that, is powerful enough to stop the pain. Therefore, if one day you go to the doctor and suddenly he says, "Oh, you have cancer," or something like that, or you begin to have pain, what I recommend you do is immediately start meditating on bodhicitta. That's the immediate medicine you should take.

Remember the story I told before, about Getsul Tsimbulwa and the awful-looking, dirty woman whose body was covered with leprosy sores? How did it happen that at first she appeared ordinary, disease-ridden, untouchable, and moments later in the pure aspect of the deity? At first, the monk's mind was obscured by negative karma and because of that impure mind he could see her only as an ordinary suffering woman and not as the enlightened being that she was. But because he felt such unbearable compassion for her suffering and completely gave himself up to offer her service, all his heavy negative karma was purified then and there, in the middle of the river, and immediately his view of her changed completely and he could see her as an enlightened being. His view became totally pure and she took him to her pure land, where he himself became enlightened. Thus you can see how powerful compassion is for purifying negative karma, purifying the mind.

Now I'd like to say a few words about the benefits of retreat.

Why do we do retreats?

We retreat in order to develop compassion. The purpose of retreat is to make our lives more beneficial, more useful for others. How? By developing the good heart. The main reason for doing retreat is to develop compassion, to realize bodhicitta, the root of the path to enlightenment, the door of the Mahayana path to enlightenment.

Even if we are reciting one mala of OM MANI PADME HUM, it is for bodhicitta, to realize bodhicitta, to develop compassion. That's what we're reciting for. Whatever other practices we do—prostrations, making offerings to Buddha, Dharma and Sangha or to statues, stupas and scriptures, or making holy objects ourselves—we do them to develop compassion, to realize bodhicitta, to be able to benefit other sentient beings. It's all for that; that's all it's for. Whatever practices we do—taking refuge, reciting the refuge prayer—the whole point is for that.

Even if we do the minimum practice of reciting one mala of OM MANI PADME HUM or we do a three year retreat or study Dharma philosophy for many years, it is all to develop compassion, to gain realizations, especially that of bodhicitta. Therefore, every single thing we do is for us to stop harming others and to benefit them. The main goal of our practice is that. If we don't stop harming others, we can't benefit them.

If you do many retreats, recite many sadhanas and chant many mantras but then in daily life retaliate the moment somebody criticizes or bothers you in some other way and try to harm that person in return, it shows that real practice is not happening. You may spend much time retreating, reciting and praying, but when it comes to dealing with other beings, the real practice, the actual practice—whose purpose is the development of patience, tolerance, compassion and loving kindness—is missing. You have not fulfilled the purpose of all the retreats, sadhanas, prayers or even that one mala of OM MANI PADME HUM that you have done. The whole, entire purpose of such practices is to help you in your daily life when dealing with other sentient beings—to not harm but benefit them. How? By developing in your mind loving kindness, compassion and bodhicitta; to develop patience, tolerance and the rest.

Therefore, especially when you are driving your car and somebody cuts you off, swerves in front of you or doesn't follow the law, when another driver honks his horn or gets angry at you, it is good to think, "If I get angry or upset, what's the point of all the practice I've been doing? If I can't practice patience, why have I recited all these mantras? What's been the purpose of my having met the Buddhadharma? What have all my retreats and prayers been for?" It's very useful to think like this. If you haven't changed your mind, your practice has had no meaning. If you think about it deeply, this is how you'll feel.

If you ask yourself, "If I don't practice patience, why am I doing all this? What for? What have I been doing all these years? What's been the purpose of reciting even one mala of OM MANI PADME HUM?" it will help calm your mind, especially on such occasions. Then, when you're able to remember that all your practices are mainly to protect your mind in everyday life, to subdue your mind so that you don't harm but only benefit others—when you can reflect in this way and practice tolerance in a situation where normally you'd get angry—when in place of anger you can arouse strong compassion for others, that's a day for great celebration.

The day you feel compassion instead of anger is truly your birthday—your great birthday for liberation, for enlightenment, for benefiting and not harming other sentient beings; a day for great celebration. Such moments are very important occasions as far as your enlightenment is concerned; very, very precious opportunities to meet the challenge of practicing Dharma.

Similarly, if somebody abuses you or does something else that normally you would find hard to deal with, couldn't stand, would make you angry and upset, and you are able to overcome your delusion of anger, you have won; you have defeated your enemy.

From the point of view of ordinary people in the mundane world, you *should* get angry; you have a right to get angry. Anger is regarded as positive. In the same way, they regard being selfish as the right way to be, something you *must* do. However, the only selfishness you should allow yourself is the selfishness of caring for other sentient beings, of benefiting other sentient beings. *That* is the right way to be; that is good selfishness. Being selfish for your own benefit opens the door to all problems; being selfish for the sake of others, caring for others, opens the door to all happiness.

Also, if you have compassion, a good heart, even if you have no external wealth, your life is rich; you are a really wealthy person. No matter how much external wealth you have, if your heart is empty of goodness, if you do not have a warm heart, if there's no compassion for others, you're poor; inner poverty makes you a real beggar.

Therefore, whether you are ordained or lay, doing lots of retreat or none, finding lots of time to study Dharma or none, the most important way to live your life is with compassion. Living with compassion is the very essence of life, the best life to lead, the most important thing you can do. Even if you are able to study Dharma your entire life—all the scriptures, sutra, tantra, everything—if your heart is empty, like an empty vessel, empty of good qualities, your whole life is empty. Even though you might have a vast intellectual understanding of Buddhism and can explain or recite the entire canon of the Buddha's sutras and tantras, if there's no compassion in your heart, your life is empty of meaning.

Even if you do one retreat after another, live in a cave without coming out or seeing other people for fifty, sixty, seventy years, even if you spend your entire life in retreat, if your heart is empty of the satisfaction that comes from cutting the thought of the eight worldly dharmas, empty of compassion for others, your life is not meaningful. Even if you put yourself in a cave without windows or doors and chant mantras for fifty or a hundred years, if your heart is empty of compassion for others, your life has no meaning.

For example, if you do prostrations with the attitude that you are prostrating for others, if in your heart you feel that you are prostrating for the hell beings, the hungry ghosts, the animals, other humans, the suras and asuras, if you feel in your heart that you're prostrating for others, even if you do only three prostrations, you feel so happy, so satisfied, that it's so worthwhile. Even though you do only three prostrations, at least they're for others. In your mind there's no tension; you feel free. In your heart, you enjoy them; your attitude is relaxed, peaceful and happy.

If, on the other hand, your attitude is that you are doing these prostrations for yourself—for *you* not to be reborn in hell and so forth—that is not so enjoyable. If you compare it with the other attitude—doing just three prostrations for others—you are not really happy. There's a big difference in the nature of your mental attitude; you are not as happy and relaxed as when you prostrate for others.

There's also a great difference from the aspect of motivation. When you dedicate each prostration to others, with each one you collect merit, good karma, like the limitless sky. When the attitude in your heart is, "I'm doing this for me not to be born in hell, for me not to suffer in the lower realms," your purpose is very limited, mean. Your purpose—for yourself not to be born in the lower realms—is so tiny, so limited, and therefore the benefits of the prostrations you do are correspondingly tiny, limited.

Hence there's a big difference between those two attitudes. Even though your motivation is still Dharma—because you are working for the happiness of your next life—the difference is huge. In other words, when you recite one Vajrasattva mantra or one mala of OM MANI PADME HUM, you should feel in your heart that it is all for the benefit of other sentient beings. The purpose behind it is that. In that way, when, with bodhicitta in your heart, you feel that each Vajrasattva mantra is for others, each one becomes 100,000 Vajrasattva mantras.

If each mantra you recite is done just for yourself to achieve the ever-lasting happiness of liberation from samsara or to have better future lives, happiness in future lives for yourself alone, it does not bring skies of merit. You lose out on that. Because you fail to generate bodhicitta motivation, you miss out on each mantra's becoming 100,000. Even though your recitation becomes a Dharma action because your motivation is virtuous—thinking of yourself not suffering in the lower realms, working for the happiness of your future lives—no matter how many Vajrasattva or OM MANI PADME HUM mantras you recite, when you compare their benefits to those you would have gained had you recited the mantras with bodhicitta, they are still kind of meaningless, wasted.

The purpose of emphasizing bodhicitta motivation at the beginning of every retreat session, repeating it again and again, is to remind you to generate bodhicitta so that you don't waste the Vajrasattva mantras you recite. It's extremely important. Constant repetition helps you understand how important bodhicitta motivation is and to remember to generate it every session.

Of course, at this point my mind has degenerated completely, but in the past, if I found that I had recited one mala of mantras without bodhicitta, I would feel that I had wasted that whole mala and would repeat it with the proper motivation.

When you have a compassionate attitude, you have peace and happiness in your life right now. No matter with whom you find yourself, you are happy and comfortable. When you have compassion for others, you are happy to be with any sentient being. Even if you live alone, you are happy. There is happiness and comfort now, and this attitude has the best future. Not only that, but you also die in the best way. If you die with compassion, your mind will be happy and peaceful and you'll die with no regret or guilt. The best way to die is with compassion for others.

Also, if you want to be reborn in a pure land, dying with compassion is the best way of making it happen. If you die with compassion, not only will your death be peaceful and happy but you will also receive good rebirths in all your coming future lives, liberation from samsara and full enlightenment—all the infinite good qualities of the buddha's holy body, speech and mind will be yours, and you will be able to enlighten numberless sentient beings.

With compassion, both your present and your future lives are happy.

Lama Zopa Rinpoche gave this teaching 6 March 1999.

Deer Park, Wisconsin, 2008

· · · 4 · · ·

The Benefits of Bodhicitta

THE SUTRA *Do-de phal-po che,*[9] which contains teachings on bodhicitta, says, "The holy, altruistic mind of enlightenment, that
purest of attitudes, is a treasury of merits."

The *Guide to the Bodhisattva's Way of Life* says, "How can one measure
the merits one collects by generating the precious thought that is the
cause of all happiness of all transmigratory beings and the medicine
that cures the suffering of all sentient beings?"[10]

From where does every single happiness, both temporary and ultimate, of every single sentient being come? From bodhicitta. What is the
one medicine for every suffering that sentient beings experience? That,
too, is bodhicitta. Therefore, there's no limit to the benefits of bodhicitta; there's no way to realize how much merit you can collect with
it. You can't say it's this much; it's immeasurable. The merits you can
collect with bodhicitta are numberless. That is the straight translation—
"How can the merits collected by generating the precious thought that
is the cause of the happiness of all transmigratory beings and the medicine for the suffering of all sentient beings be measured?"

With the mind of bodhicitta, each breath in and each breath out

[9] *Buddhavatamsaka Sutra*
[10] Chapter 1, verse 26

become a cause for the happiness of all sentient beings. With this purest of attitudes, bodhicitta, every breath you take benefits each sentient being and with each breath, with every action, you create skies of merit.

Therefore, if you want to accumulate the conditions necessary for attaining realizations on the path to enlightenment, you should put all your effort into developing your own precious mind of bodhicitta.

When you think of fulfilling your wishes, it's not suffering you want. Normally, you don't wish for suffering. What you wish for is happiness. Of course, the happiness that most of us wish for is actually suffering; what we usually think of as happiness is not pure happiness. However, as far as what we wish for is concerned, from the side of the wish, what we are looking for is happiness, not suffering.

That said, every single happiness—from that of full enlightenment, through liberation from samsara and the happiness of future lives, down to even the happiness of this life—depends on merit, good karma. Without good karma, nothing works. Without good karma, the cause of happiness, you can't enjoy even the slightest happiness. Without merit, there's no comfort; everything depends on merit. Realizations of the path, temporary happiness, even the work of this life, such as success in business—every single thing depends on merit. So, what's the best way to collect extensive merit? It's by practicing bodhicitta, meditating on bodhicitta.

Also, the merit you collect with bodhicitta is inexhaustible, unceasing. It doesn't stop until you reach enlightenment, and even after you reach enlightenment it continues. You continuously experience the result; your mind remains in the state of peerless happiness. Not only that. As a result of the merits you collect with bodhicitta, you liberate numberless other sentient beings and bring them to full enlightenment. Without discriminating, you bring sentient beings equaling the sky, every single one, to the full enlightenment of buddhahood.

The teachings say that merits collected without bodhicitta are like a "water tree." I think that means a banana tree—the fruit comes, you use it once and the tree no longer bears fruit. In other words, if merit is created without bodhicitta, you experience the result once and it's finished. Merit collected with bodhicitta is completely different—you enjoy it all the time, lifetime after lifetime, and even after you achieve enlightenment, you keep enjoying it. Such merit is inexhaustible.

That's why you should put all your daily life's effort, everything you do, into developing bodhicitta. Whether you are happy or unhappy, whether you encounter problems or are problem-free, whatever your circumstances, favorable or unfavorable, whatever conditions you find yourself in, you must put every single effort into this, into living your life with the attitude of bodhicitta.

Now, when you do the Vajrasattva sadhana or other practices, even though they begin with bodhicitta motivation, when you come to the mantra recitation, *again*, just before you begin to recite the mantra, dedicate very precisely by thinking, "Each mantra I recite is for every hell being, each mantra is for every hungry ghost, each mantra is for every animal, each mantra is for every human, each mantra is for every sura, asura and intermediate state being."

Even though you begin the practice with bodhicitta motivation, make sure that when you come to the actual recitation of the mantra it is directed more to the benefit of others than yourself. Make sure that instead of feeling in your heart that it is "I, me" for whom you are reciting the mantra, you feel that you are doing it for others. Make sure very precisely that each mantra you recite is for others, not yourself. Instead of filling your heart with "I," fill your heart with others. Begin your mantra recitation like that; during the session, recite the mantra with as much bodhicitta as you can generate; and every now and then, check your motivation to make sure that your attitude is that of more concern for others than yourself. If it's not, fix it.

If you want to be a lucky person, if you want good luck in your life, bodhicitta is the best way to create the good luck you desire. If you want to be lucky, put all your effort into practicing bodhicitta all the time. If you are a good hearted person you are truly lucky because gradually all your wishes get fulfilled—your wishes for your own welfare and your wishes for the welfare of others. You can stop all your defilements, your mental stains and errors, and accomplish all realizations, enabling you to liberate others from suffering and do perfect work for other sentient beings. Your good heart allows you to accomplish your own aims and those of others. That's the definition of a really lucky person—one who has compassion for others, loving kindness, bodhicitta.

It also says in the *Guide to the Bodhisattva's Way of Life*, "Since merely thinking of benefiting others transcends making offerings to all the buddhas, what need is there to say how extraordinary it is to actually attempt to bring happiness to every single sentient being without exception?"[11]

Here Shantideva is saying that even *thinking* of benefiting others is much higher, more special, much greater and more extraordinary than

[11] Chapter 1, verse 27

making offerings to all the buddhas. Therefore, if you go beyond this extremely beneficial thought and actually *try* to bring happiness to all sentient beings without exception, actually *work* for their happiness, what need is there to say how extraordinarily beneficial this is, how far it surpasses making offerings to all buddhas?

Also, in his commentary to Maitreya Buddha's teachings, *Do-de-gyän* [*Mahayanasutralamkara*], Arya Asanga says that benefiting one sentient being is more meaningful than making offerings to buddhas and bodhisattvas equaling in number the atoms of the world. How can it be that benefiting one sentient being is more meaningful than making offerings to not just one buddha but to buddhas equaling in number the atoms of the world?

This is incredible advice, similar to that given by Shantideva when he was talking about the benefits of bodhicitta, how extraordinary it is merely to think of benefiting others. For example, when we generate bodhicitta motivation, the thought of achieving enlightenment for sentient beings, the thought of benefiting sentient beings, merely this thought, just this wish, is greater than making offerings to all the buddhas.

Helping others is an offering to the buddhas

I mentioned before that when we help sentient beings we can also think of it as an offering to the buddhas. This is a very useful way to think.

There are many ways in which we can help sentient beings. I'm not just talking about our pet dogs and cats—and whether we keep them for their happiness or ours is also a question—but also insects. Actually,

perhaps we should also keep insects as pets—mosquitoes, spiders . . .
especially the ones we don't like! Anyway, whatever sentient being we
benefit—domestic animals, insects, hell beings, pretas, people—and
whichever way we help them—for example, giving a Dharma talk to
help somebody with depression or some other mental problem, medicine for illness or food or money to a beggar—sincerely trying to help
either physically or mentally, we can always combine two things: making charity to that sentient being and an offering to all the buddhas.

If, for example, you give food or money to a beggar, you're giving
immediate help to that sentient being but at the same time it becomes
the best kind of offering to the buddhas and bodhisattvas of the ten
directions. Why? Because what the buddhas and bodhisattvas cherish
all the time is sentient beings; nobody else. They are constantly working
for sentient beings, cherishing only sentient beings. Therefore, when
you help sentient beings you are helping the numberless buddhas and
bodhisattvas. That's the reality.

Even if you don't think that your helping a sentient being is an offering to the buddhas and bodhisattvas, in fact it becomes the best kind of
offering you can make, the most pleasing offering possible. As I also
mentioned before, even though you don't directly help the parents,
when you help their children you make the parents happy, because what
they cherish most in their lives, what they hold most dear in their hearts,
is their children.

Similarly, if you harm a child you harm its parents, and in the same
way, therefore, if you harm sentient beings you harm the buddhas and
bodhisattvas; it displeases them greatly.

A child is like its parents' life, or heart, and the buddhas and bodhisattvas cherish sentient beings in the same way. Therefore, if you do good things for sentient beings, if you benefit them, offer service to them, you are not only offering service to all the buddhas and bodhisattvas but the very best kind of service.

Thinking like this helps you practice tolerance, or patience. It helps you to not get angry at other sentient beings, to not arouse ill-will, to avoid hurting or harming them. It is very helpful. Inflicting pain upon a sentient being is like inflicting pain upon the buddhas and bodhisattvas. That's not to say they experience pain in the same way that we suffering sentient beings do but it is certainly displeasing.

Therefore, when you offer service to a child or an old person, when you give things to others, for example, when you make charity to a beggar or even throw a party for others and offer them food and drink, remember that you are also making an offering to the buddhas and bodhisattvas. If you are aware of this, if when you give to the sentient being you also intentionally think you are making an offering to the buddhas and bodhisattvas, you combine two things. The sentient beings derive benefit from whatever you have given them and you collect merit by making an offering to the buddhas and bodhisattvas with your intentional thought.

If, at such times, you consciously think, "By helping this sentient being I am also making an offering to the buddhas and bodhisattvas," if you remember that what you are doing with this sentient being also affects the buddhas and bodhisattvas, that doing something good pleases them, two things get done and you collect much more merit than you would have by simply making an offering, thinking of only the Buddha.

When you make charity, whether it's an offering to monks, monasteries or refugees, homeless people or the sick, at that time remember that you are also making offerings to the buddhas and bodhisattvas; you are giving to sentient beings but offering to the buddhas and bodhisattvas. In this way you collect far more merit, an unbelievable amount.

The sutra *Do-de phal-po che* says, "The holy, purest thought of enlightenment is a treasury of merit (or fortune); from this come the buddhas of the three times."

This means that numberless past, numberless present and numberless future buddhas have all come from bodhicitta, that holy, most pure thought of enlightenment. The text goes on, "From this [bodhicitta] comes the happiness of all the world's transmigrators."

The Tibetan phrase here is *di-lä jig-ten dro-wa kun-gyi de-wa jung. Di-lä* means "from this." The next term, *jig-ten*, requires a little more explanation.

The meaning of "jig-ten"

The sense is "change," but to make it clearer we should say "changeable aggregates." We also have the term *jig* in one of the six root delusions, the one called five wrong views, *ta-wa nga-ta ta-min nga.* One of those is *jig-tsog-la ta-wa,* the view of the changeable aggregates. Here, *jig* is the same, meaning change. *Ta-wa* itself simply means view, but the implication here is wrong view, so together it becomes something like changeable wrong view. *Jig-tsog-wa* means changeable collection. What is that changeable collection? It is the five aggregates.

How does ignorance, the root of samsara, arise? How does that ignorance, which is the wrong view of the *jig-tsog-la* happen?

First, we have *mig-kyen*, the objective condition. The mind looks at the aggregates, which are impermanent and therefore changeable in nature, and labels them "I." The thought thinks of the transitory aggregates and makes up the label "I," the merely imputed I. But this I, which is merely imputed by that thought, doesn't appear back to the mind as merely imputed. At that moment, you are not aware that the I is merely imputed by the mind.

Right after the I has been merely imputed by the mind, the negative imprints left on the consciousness by past ignorance, the concept of inherent existence, immediately *project* that the merely imputed I is inherently existent. Right after your mind merely imputes the I, just like imprints left on a film in a camera, the imprints left on the mental continuum by past ignorance—not just any ignorance, but the ignorance of inherent existence—immediately *project* the hallucination of inherent existence onto that merely imputed I. Buddhas cannot see this inherent existence; bodhisattvas who realize emptiness can't see it; and when you analyze, even you can't find it—because it doesn't exist. What those buddhas and bodhisattvas see is a *non*-inherently existent I. That's what they see.

However, with us, as soon as our thought merely labels I, in the very next moment, that merely imputed I appears back to the same continuity of thought as *not* merely labeled by mind, as existing from its own side. The very next moment of mind apprehends, "Oh, that's true, that's a real I there." So, that real I appearing as true, seeing that real I appearing from there as true, is the wrong view, *ta-wa*.

Now you can understand the meaning of *jig-tsog-la ta-wa* a little better. *Jig-tsog* means changeable collection, in other words, the aggregates; *ta-wa* means view. When the next thought moment of the same continuity of the thought that merely imputed the I *believes*, or apprehends, that what is appearing to it is true, is something real from its own side, then at that time the *jig-tsog-la ta-wa*, the wrong view, happened. This wrong view is established on the aggregates, which are changeable by nature—like a table-cloth covering a table.

You can see the evolution, but since the wrong view is of the I, why does the term contain the aggregates, *jig-tsog*—the changeable collection (*tsog* means collection), the changeable aggregates? Why are they mentioned here, what's the connection?

Well, by understanding the evolution of the wrong view, you can see why. By thinking of the aggregates, your mind labels I. First you think of the *base* and then you apply the label. The cause, or reason, for the mind applying a label has to come before the label; the reason, or cause, of the label has to come before the label. They don't come together; the cause comes first. So, why is the particular label I chosen? Because first the base is identified, then the appropriate label applied.

It's the same with any phenomenon. By looking at the base, thinking of the base, seeing the base, hearing, touching, smelling or tasting the base, the mind that experiences the base and then creates the label, this or that. Depending on the base, the thought makes up the label and that's how all phenomena come into existence, happen.

Abbreviating *jig-tsog-la ta-wa*, the view of the changeable aggregates, we say *jig-ta*. *Jig* means change and *ta* means view, but although literally it comes to changeable, or transitory, view, that's not what it means. It is not the view that is changeable or transitory; the view is of the I. Change refers to the aggregates; the view is to do with the I.

Why am I describing ignorance here? Why, along with the wrong view, are the aggregates brought up? If you think of the evolution, you can understand. But now I should finish discussing the quotation from the sutra.

"From this comes the happiness of all the world's transmigrators"— the term here is *jig-ten dro-wa*, so perhaps it should be translated as "transmigratory beings dependent on change," since *jig-ten* means dependent on change.

It means that the I, the being, exists by depending on the aggregates. That's what the "change" refers to. It means aggregates, which are transitory in nature, *jig-ten*. It really depends on the context. Actually, *jig-ten* is a general term that means both the world and its inhabitants—not only the place but also the beings that live there. It depends on the context. Usually it means suffering beings, *jig-ten*; samsaric beings, *jig-ten-lä de-pa* and *jig-ten-pa*—"those beings who are beyond dependence on change" and "those beings who are dependent on change," respectively. In this context, *jig-ten-pa* means samsaric beings, "those who are dependent on change," and *jig-ten-lä de-pa* means "those who have gone beyond samsara and are not suffering beings dependent on the aggregates," which are changeable in nature, suffering in nature, that is, samsara. So *jig-ten-lä de-pa* means those who are beyond *jig-ten*.

Here, *ten* means dependent on something; those who are dependent on change, which means the aggregates, transitory in nature, but also suffering in nature—that means samsara. Thus, *jig-ten-pa* means beings that are dependent on change, which means the aggregates. The aggregates are changeable in nature, suffering—that's samsara. The aggregates are samsara.

"From this, the happiness of all the transmigratory beings dependent on change"—*jig-ten dro-wa*, dependent on change. That describes the aggregates, samsara. Beings who are dependent on the aggregates, which are changeable and suffering in nature—that's samsara, the continuity of which circles from one life to the next. Beings that are dependent on that are called samsaric beings, circlers.

The next line says, "From this, *all* good things, all goodness praised by the victorious ones comes" or "From this, one receives *all* the goodness praised by the victorious ones." It can be translated either way.

From bodhicitta, there is no doubt that you can become a buddha, one who is the victor over, who has conquered, defeated, destroyed, not only the delusions but even the subtle negative imprints of delusion. So, "From this, there is no doubt that you can become the principal victorious one"—amongst holy beings, the principal one, buddha, the most perfect of beings.

The next line: "With this, the defilements of all the *jig-ten* will cease." Here, the *jig-ten* can mean all worldly beings. You can say, "All the defilements of worldly beings will cease," but to my mind—I don't know how it sounds to others—worldly has the connotation of "not being free from worldly concern, attachment clinging to this life." Such beings are worldly beings, those who have not renounced attachment to this life. To me, "worldly being" has more this meaning than "samsaric being," although here, worldly means samsaric. The Tibetan is *di-ni jig-ten kun-gyi drib-pa se-par-gyur*—"With this [bodhicitta], the defilements of all the *jig-ten* will cease" is the word-for-word translation—the meaning is the defilements of all samsaric beings or, you can say, the defilements of all the beings dependent on change, which means the aggregates, as we discussed above. All these defilements will cease.

On the other hand, I'm not completely sure what *jig-ten* refers to because even *arya* beings, like arhats, higher bodhisattvas and buddhas as well, exist by depending on aggregates. Even those who are free from samsara but still have subtle defilements—like arhats and higher bodhisattvas—exist in dependence upon aggregates. Not aggregates that are suffering in nature but those that are changeable in nature. Those who are free from samsara, arhats, don't experience suffering, but they do depend upon changeable aggregates, *jig-ten*. So I'm not sure how widely the term *jig-ten* extends. Usually it means just samsaric beings but perhaps it can also cover those who still have subtle defilements—arhats and higher bodhisattvas.

The benefits of your own bodhicitta

While this quotation from *Do-de phal-po che* explains the incredible benefits of bodhicitta in general, you can also use it to think of the extensive benefits that come from your own bodhicitta. Thus, your own holy mind of bodhicitta is the treasury of all merit. Of course, you can't relate the buddhas of the three times to your own bodhicitta, but they all do come from bodhicitta in general. Like numberless past, present and future buddhas arose from Guru Shakyamuni Buddha's bodhicitta—not *all*, but numberless—you can relate to it like that. The happiness of numberless transmigrators dependent on change comes from *your* bodhicitta.

The happiness of all migratory beings comes from bodhicitta in general, but with *your* bodhicitta, you can still bring much happiness—the happiness of this life, future lives, liberation and enlightenment—to numberless sentient beings. Your bodhicitta can cause numberless hell beings, numberless hungry ghosts, numberless animals, numberless humans, numberless suras, numberless asuras and numberless intermediate state beings to experience all happiness up to enlightenment. All that comes from *your* bodhicitta, is caused by *your* bodhicitta.

You can even think very specifically. For example, your, one person's, bodhicitta causes numberless ants to experience all temporary and ultimate happiness up to enlightenment. Think how many ants you can find at just one spot, how many thousands there are in a nest under a rock. There are so many more in a field or on a mountain. There's no question how many more there are in one country. Like that, if you expand from one spot and think how many ants there are in this world, this universe, numberless universes, you can realize how many there are and how your bodhicitta brings them all happiness up to enlightenment.

Think how your, one person's, bodhicitta brings *all* happiness to numberless other insects, numberless fish in the water, numberless shellfish on the rocks, on the piles supporting piers, in this world, in this universe, in numberless universes. If you think by elaborating in this way—the numbers of shellfish, for instance, are unbelievable, countless, and your bodhicitta, the bodhicitta of one person, you, can bring all happiness to all of them—it's incredible.

Think of other sentient beings one by one. The worms in the ground

—your bodhicitta brings all happiness to numberless worms. Caterpillars, those hairy ones that walk in such long, well-disciplined straight lines—uncountable, numberless caterpillars in just one spot, let alone this universe, numberless universes—your bodhicitta brings every happiness to them all. Or on the beach there are so many tiny crabs—you can see them when the tide goes out. They make all these little holes in the sand and when they come out looking for food the seagulls try to eat them. Think how many there must be in this universe, in numberless universes. The bodhicitta of you, one person, can bring them all happiness up to enlightenment. Think how unbelievable that is.

Even without thinking about the numberless hell beings, hungry ghosts, humans and so forth but merely thinking about the different kinds of animal and how each type is numberless, it is incredible that your, one person's, bodhicitta can cause them to experience all happiness up to enlightenment and, as it says here, "With this [bodhicitta], the defilements of all those dependent on change [jig-ten, all the samsaric beings] will cease." The bodhicitta of you, one person, can eradicate the defilements of each of the numberless animals, of whom even each type is numberless. Your bodhicitta can eradicate not only their suffering but also their two types of defilement. It's unbelievable. There are so many different kinds of animal and even in this world, each one is numberless. When you think how many there must be in numberless universes and what one person's realization of bodhicitta, the good heart, can do, how much it can benefit others, it's really unbelievable.

Think how many flies there must be. Even on one cowpat there are thousands upon thousands of tiny flies keeping themselves busy, and that's just on the ground. In the air there are so many more. You don't notice them when the sun's not shining but when it's out you can see these huge clouds of flies in the air; uncountable numbers of tiny flies. From these few examples from the animal realm, just these few kinds of insect, you can understand how many suffering sentient beings there are.

Here I'm just talking about one spot on the ground but you should think of this world, then of numberless universes—how many unimaginable numbers of sentient being are suffering. Therefore if you, one person, have bodhicitta, it can stop all their gross and subtle defilements and put an end to all their suffering. That's incredible.

The only solution to suffering

There are many animals, such as snakes, tigers, leopards and so forth, whose only food is other animals. They don't eat plants; they don't live on potatoes or carrots; they don't grow vegetables. All they eat is other sentient beings. Snakes eat mice, frogs and so forth. There are many sentient beings whose only food is other sentient beings; who, due to karma, depend on killing others for their very survival. If you keep such animals as pets you have to feed them other sentient beings. For them, not eating others is suffering because they can't survive in any other way and killing others is also suffering, since by harming others they create negative karma. Tigers in zoos, for example, have to be fed goats. Anyway, there are many sentient beings like this.

A while back in Singapore, where we frequently liberate many animals—frogs, fish and so forth—we bought five snakes from a restaurant in order to liberate them. When we opened the sack they were in they couldn't crawl away immediately because they'd been sedated. It was as if they were drunk or on drugs! The thought came, if we release them, they'll eat mice, but if we hadn't freed them, they'd have become the restaurant's evening special. Either way, it's a problem. What we have to do is to free them from samsara; that's the only solution—free them from delusion and karma. Until that happens, either mode of existence in samsara—killing others or not killing others—is a problem. The only solution is to free them from samsara.

The importance of the Dharma center

Therefore we ourselves should practice Dharma as much as possible and, if we can, spread Dharma and help other people understand it. If we can help those sentient beings who have precious human bodies understand the teachings and get them to practice Dharma as much as possible, we can effect that solution right away, right now. You can't explain Dharma to snakes; you can't teach them to meditate! You can't start a meditation center for snakes, mice or tigers. You can't establish a retreat center for mosquitoes, organize retreats for mosquitoes! There's no way they can understand Dharma. Not even dogs or cats can understand it.

It's important for you to practice Dharma as much as possible yourself, to actualize the path, and to help other people, those sentient beings who have human bodies, understand Dharma; to get others to practice Dharma. Actually, it's unbelievably urgent, an emergency. The only sentient beings you can really help to understand Dharma, the path to liberation and enlightenment, are other human beings. In this way, they can avoid being reborn in the lower realms, as hell beings, hungry ghosts or animals. They don't have to be reborn as mosquitoes. They can be saved from rebirth as snakes, tigers or other harmful animals. You can liberate people from rebirth in the lower realms, where you're in danger if you try to survive and in danger if you don't.

Who can you help right now? Human beings. The only way you can help animals is by taking them around holy objects or purifying them with blessed water. You can give them a little help like that but there's no way that you can make them understand and practice Dharma. It's only human beings you can help right now.

Therefore, you should make every effort to help human beings purify their past negative karma and protect their present karma by living in vows, by abstaining from negative karma. In that way they can liberate themselves from rebirth as, for example, those harmful animals we've been talking about. Not just that, but also free themselves from samsara and bring themselves to full enlightenment.

It's essential that you practice Dharma yourself as much as you possibly can. And thus we see how very important the Dharma center is; how it plays a crucial role in saving, liberating, rescuing human beings from reincarnating back into the lower realms. The Dharma center is an emergency rescue operation, like when police go in with all that noise—sirens blaring, red and blue lights flashing, helicopters whirling—to rescue people in distress! Like that, the meditation center plays a very important role in the emergency rescue of people, human beings, using the seat belt and life jacket of the lam-rim—meditation on refuge and karma immediately saves you from falling into the lower realms again.

Then, on the basis of that, the center helps bring people to liberation from samsara and enlightenment. The meditation center, the Dharma organization, plays a very important role in this. This is the way to empty the lower realms, to ensure through Dharma that no more harmful sentient beings get born—doing sincere work with pure motivation solely for the benefit of others.

Numberless beings depend on you

Thus your bodhicitta is unbelievable. It's unbelievable how much benefit you can bring to numberless sentient beings in *each* realm. Therefore, now, you can see how crucial it is—how the happiness of numberless sentient beings depends on you, how it's in your hands. That means it depends on how much you practice bodhicitta, how much effort you exert trying to realize bodhicitta. It is crucial, *most urgent*, that you realize bodhicitta, train your mind in *this*.

Thus, the practice of bodhicitta becomes very important in your daily life. In all activities, under any circumstances—when you are happy, when you're experiencing problems—at all times, never separate from bodhicitta. Never stop wishing that all sentient beings be happy. Never lose your determination for sentient beings equaling the extent of space to have all happiness and to be free from all suffering and, in this way, to lead them all to enlightenment.

If you live your life with this attitude constantly in mind, then, if you have taken the bodhisattva vow, you are able to protect it, by the way. Even though there are many different vows enumerated, if you live your life with this attitude, you take care of all those different vows. This attitude encompasses all those vows. If you never separate from bodhicitta in all your activities, each merit you create contains the three types of bodhisattva morality and the other paramitas as well.

Lama Zopa Rinpoche gave this teaching 7 March 1999.

··· Dedication ···

[Please dedicate the merit of having read the teachings in this book as follows.]

"DUE TO ALL THE PAST, present and future merits collected by me, buddhas, bodhisattvas and all other sentient beings, may bodhicitta, the source of all the happiness and success of myself and all other sentient beings, be generated in my own mind and in the minds of all sentient beings without even one second's delay and may that which has been generated increase.

"Due to all the past, present and future merits collected by me, buddhas, bodhisattvas and all other sentient beings, may all my father-mother sentient beings have all happiness, may the three lower realms be empty forever and may all the bodhisattvas' prayers succeed immediately. May I be able to cause all this by myself alone.

"Due to all the merits of the three times collected by me, buddhas, bodhisattvas and all other sentient beings, from now on may I offer extensive benefit like the sky to all sentient beings as Lama Tsong Khapa did by having within me in all my future lifetimes the same qualities that Lama Tsong Khapa possessed.

"Due to the merits of the three times collected by me, buddhas, bodhisattvas and all other sentient beings—which appear to be real merits, existing from there, from their own side, as projected by my hallucinating mind's ignorance, but are in reality empty of that—may I—which is projected by my hallucinating mind's ignorance as a real *me*, a real self existing from there, appearing from there, but which is empty of that, empty of the hallucination of a real I appearing from there—achieve enlightenment—which appears to be a real enlightenment as projected by my hallucinating mind's ignorance but which is in fact empty of a real enlightenment appearing from there—and lead all sentient beings—which appear to me as real ones from there but which are a hallucination, a projection of my ignorance, empty of being real sentient beings appearing from there—to that enlightenment—which appears to me to be a real one from there but which is a hallucination projected by my ignorance, empty of being a real one appearing from there—by myself alone—who also appears to my mind as a real one appearing from there but which is a hallucination projected by my ignorance, which means that this me, this I, is totally empty of a real one appearing from there.

"May Lama Tsong Khapa's complete path to be actualized within my mind and within the minds of my family members and all students and benefactors of this organization, spread and flourish in all directions, and may I be able to cause these teachings to be actualized in the minds of all sentient beings by myself alone."

The Foundation of All Good Qualities

The foundation of all good qualities is the kind and perfect,
    pure Guru;
Correct devotion to him is the root of the path.
By clearly seeing this and applying great effort,
Please bless me to rely upon him with great respect.

Understanding that the precious freedom of this rebirth is found
    only once,
Is greatly meaningful, and is difficult to find again,
Please bless me to generate the mind that unceasingly,
Day and night, takes its essence.

This life is as impermanent as a water bubble;
Remember how quickly it decays and death comes.
After death, just like a shadow follows the body,
The results of black and white karma follow.

Finding firm and definite conviction in this,
Please bless me always to be careful
To abandon even the slightest negativities
And accomplish all virtuous deeds.

Seeking samsaric pleasures is the door to all suffering:
They are uncertain and cannot be relied upon.

Recognizing these shortcomings,
Please bless me to generate the strong wish for the bliss of liberation.

Led by this pure thought,
Mindfulness, alertness, and great caution arise.
The root of the teachings is keeping the pratimoksha vows:
Please bless me to accomplish this essential practice.

Just as I have fallen into the sea of samsara,
So have all mother migratory beings.
Please bless me to see this, train in supreme bodhichitta,
And bear the responsibility of freeing migratory beings.

Even if I develop only bodhichitta, but I don't practice the three
        types of morality,
I will not achieve enlightenment.
With my clear recognition of this,
Please bless me to practice the bodhisattva vows with great energy.

Once I have pacified distractions to wrong objects
And correctly analyzed the meaning of reality,
Please bless me to generate quickly within my mindstream
The unified path of calm abiding and special insight.

Having become a pure vessel by training in the general path,
Please bless me to enter
The holy gateway of the fortunate ones:
The supreme vajra vehicle.

At that time, the basis of accomplishing the two attainments
Is keeping pure vows and samaya.
As I have become firmly convinced of this,
Please bless me to protect these vows and pledges like my life.

Then, having realized the importance of the two stages,
The essence of the Vajrayana,
By practicing with great energy, never giving up the four sessions,
Please bless me to realize the teachings of the holy Guru.

Like that, may the gurus who show the noble path
And the spiritual friends who practice it have long lives.
Please bless me to pacify completely
All outer and inner hindrances.

In all my lives, never separated from perfect gurus,
May I enjoy the magnificent Dharma.
By completing the qualities of the stages and paths,
May I quickly attain the state of Vajradhara.

Colophon
This lam-rim prayer by Lama Tsongkhapa, translated by Jampäl Lhundrup,
comes from Essential Buddhist Prayers: An FPMT Prayer Book,
Volume 1, 2008

··· Appendix 2 ···

Practicing Guru Devotion with the Nine Attitudes

I am requesting the kind lord root guru,
Who is more extraordinary than all the buddhas:
Please bless me to be able to devote myself to the qualified lord guru
With great respect in all my future lifetimes.

By realizing that correctly devoting myself to the kind lord guru—
Who is the foundation of all good qualities—
Is the root of happiness and goodness,
I shall devote myself to him with great respect,
Not forsaking him even at the cost of my life.

Thinking of the importance of the qualified guru,
May I allow myself to enter under his control.

May I be like an obedient son,
Acting exactly in accordance with the guru's advice.

Even when maras, evil friends and the like
Try to split me from the guru,
May I be like a vajra, inseparable forever.

When the guru gives me work, whatever the burden,
May I be like the earth, carrying all.

When I devote myself to the guru,
Whatever suffering occurs (hardships or problems),
May I be like a mountain, immovable.
(The mind should not be upset or discouraged.)

Even if I have to perform all the unpleasant tasks,
May I be like a servant of the king,
With a mind undisturbed.

May I abandon pride.
Holding myself lower than the guru,
May I be like a sweeper.

May I be like a rope, joyfully holding the guru's work,
No matter how difficult or heavy a burden,

Even when the guru criticizes, provokes or ignores me,
May I be like a dog without anger,
Never responding with anger.

May I be like a (ferry) boat,
Never upset at any time to come or go for the guru.

O glorious and precious root guru,
Please bless me to be able to practice in this way.
From now on, in all my future lifetimes,
May I be able to devote myself to the guru in this way.

· · · · ·

By reciting these words aloud and reflecting on their meaning in your mind, you will have the good fortune to be able to devote yourself correctly to the precious guru from life to life in all your future lifetimes. If you offer service and respect and make offerings to the precious guru with these nine attitudes, even if you do not practice intentionally you will develop many good qualities, collect extensive merit and quickly achieve full enlightenment.

Note: the words in parentheses are not to be read aloud. They have been added to clarify the text and should be kept in mind but not recited.

Colophon
Composed by Shabkar Tsogdrug Rangdrol; translated by Lama Zopa Rinpoche; scribed by Lillian Too and Ven. Thubten Dekyong (Tsenla), February 1999 at Kachoe Dechen Ling, Aptos, California; edited by Nicholas Ribush and Ven. Connie Miller.

··· References ···

Shantideva. *A Guide to the Bodhisattva Way of Life (Bodhicaryavatara)*. Translated by Vesna A. Wallace & B. Alan Wallace. Ithaca: Snow Lion Publications, 1997.

Zopa Rinpoche, Lama Thubten. *Daily Purification: A Short Vajrasattva Meditation*. Edited by Nicholas Ribush. Boston: Lama Yeshe Wisdom Archive, 2001.

———. *Making Life Meaningful*. Edited by Nicholas Ribush. Boston: Lama Yeshe Wisdom Archive, 2001.

———. *Teachings from the Vajrasattva Retreat*. Edited by Ailsa Cameron & Nicholas Ribush. Boston: Lama Yeshe Wisdom Archive, 2000.

LAMA YESHE WISDOM ARCHIVE

The LAMA YESHE WISDOM ARCHIVE (LYWA) is the collected works of Lama Thubten Yeshe and Lama Thubten Zopa Rinpoche. Lama Zopa Rinpoche, its spiritual director, founded the ARCHIVE in 1996.

Lama Yeshe and Lama Zopa Rinpoche began teaching at Kopan Monastery, Nepal, in 1970. Since then, their teachings have been recorded and transcribed. At present we have well over 10,000 hours of digital audio and some 70,000 pages of raw transcript. Many recordings, mostly teachings by Lama Zopa Rinpoche, remain to be transcribed, and as Rinpoche continues to teach, the number of recordings in the ARCHIVE increases accordingly. Most of our transcripts have been neither checked nor edited.

Here at the LYWA we are making every effort to organize the transcription of that which has not yet been transcribed, edit that which has not yet been edited, and generally do the many other tasks detailed below.

The work of the LAMA YESHE WISDOM ARCHIVE falls into two categories: archiving and dissemination.

Archiving requires managing the recordings of teachings by Lama Yeshe and Lama Zopa Rinpoche that have already been collected, collecting recordings of teachings given but not yet sent to the ARCHIVE, and collecting recordings of Lama Zopa's on-going teachings, talks, advice and so forth as he travels the world for the benefit of all. Incoming media are then catalogued and stored safely while being kept accessible for further work.

We organize the transcription of audio, add the transcripts to the already existent database of teachings, manage this database, have transcripts checked, and make transcripts available to editors or others doing research on or practicing these teachings.

Other archiving activities include working with video and photographs of the Lamas and digitizing ARCHIVE materials.

Dissemination involves making the Lamas' teachings available through various avenues including books for free distribution and sale, lightly edited transcripts, a monthly e-letter (see below), DVDs, articles in *Mandala* and other magazines and on our website. Irrespective of the medium we choose, the teachings require a significant amount of work to prepare them for distribution.

This is just a summary of what we do. The ARCHIVE was established with virtually no seed funding and has developed solely through the kindness of many people, some of whom we have mentioned at the front of this book and most of the others on our website. We sincerely thank them all.

Our further development similarly depends upon the generosity of those who see the benefit and necessity of this work, and we would be extremely grateful for your help. Thus we hereby appeal to you for your kind support. If you would like to make a contribution to help us with any of the above tasks or to sponsor books for free distribution, please contact us:

LAMA YESHE WISDOM ARCHIVE
PO Box 636, Lincoln, MA 01773, USA
Telephone (781) 259-4466; Fax (678) 868-4806
info@LamaYeshe.com
www.LamaYeshe.com

The LAMA YESHE WISDOM ARCHIVE is a 501(c)(3) tax-deductible, non-profit corporation dedicated to the welfare of all sentient beings and totally dependent upon your donations for its continued existence. Thank you so much for your support. You may contribute by mailing a check, bank draft or money order to our Weston address; by making a donation on our secure website; by mailing us your credit card number or phoning it in; or by transferring funds directly to our bank—ask us for details.

LAMA YESHE WISDOM ARCHIVE MEMBERSHIP

In order to raise the money we need to employ editors to make available the thousands of hours of teachings mentioned above, we have established a membership plan. Membership costs US$1,000 and its main benefit is that you will be helping make the Lamas' incredible teachings available to a worldwide audience. More direct and tangible benefits to you personally include free Lama Yeshe and Lama Zopa Rinpoche books from the ARCHIVE and Wisdom Publications, a year's subscription to *Mandala*, a year of monthly pujas by the monks and nuns at Kopan Monastery with your personal dedication, and access to an exclusive members-only section of our website containing special, unpublished teachings currently unavailable to others. Please see www.LamaYeshe.com for more information.

MONTHLY E-LETTER

Each month we send out a free e-letter containing our latest news and a previously unpublished teaching by Lama Yeshe or Lama Zopa Rinpoche. To see nearly eighty back-issues or to subscribe with your email address, please go to our website.

The Foundation for the Preservation of the Mahayana Tradition

The Foundation for the Preservation of the Mahayana Tradition (FPMT) is an international organization of Buddhist meditation study and retreat centers, both urban and rural, monasteries, publishing houses, healing centers and other related activities founded in 1975 by Lama Thubten Yeshe and Lama Thubten Zopa Rinpoche. At present, there are more than 160 FPMT activities in over thirty countries worldwide.

The FPMT has been established to facilitate the study and practice of Mahayana Buddhism in general and the Tibetan Gelug tradition, founded in the fifteenth century by the great scholar, yogi and saint, Lama Je Tsongkhapa, in particular.

Every quarter, the Foundation publishes a wonderful news journal, *Mandala*, from its International Office in the United States of America. To subscribe or view back issues, please go to the *Mandala* website, www.mandalamagazine.org, or contact:

FPMT
1632 SE 11th Avenue, Portland, OR 97214
Telephone (503) 808-1588; Fax (503) 808-1589
info@fpmt.org
www.fpmt.org

The FPMT website also offers teachings by His Holiness the Dalai Lama, Lama Yeshe, Lama Zopa Rinpoche and many other highly respected teachers in the tradition, details about the FPMT's educational programs, audio through FPMT radio, a link to the excellent FPMT Store, a complete listing of FPMT centers all over the world and in your area, and links to FPMT centers on the web, where you will find details of their programs, and to other interesting Buddhist and Tibetan home pages.

Discovering Buddhism at Home or Online

Awakening the limitless potential of your mind,
achieving all peace and happiness

Over 2500 years ago, Shakyamuni Buddha gained direct insight into the nature of reality, perfected the qualities of wisdom, compassion, and power, and revealed the path to his disciples. In the 11th Century, Atisha brought these teachings to Tibet in the form of the lam-rim—the stages on the path to enlightenment. The lam-rim tradition found its pinnacle in the teachings of the great Tibetan saint Je Tsongkhapa in the 14th Century, and these teachings continued to pass from teacher to student up to this present day.

When Lama Thubten Yeshe and Lama Zopa Rinpoche transmitted these teachings to their disciples, they imparted a deeply experiential tradition of study and practice, leading thousands of seekers to discover the truth of what the Buddha taught. This tradition is the core of *Discovering Buddhism*—a two-year, fourteen-module series that provides a solid foundation in the teachings and practice of Tibetan Mahayana Buddhism.

How it Works: Each *Discovering Buddhism* module consists of teachings, meditations and practices, readings, assessment questions, and a short retreat. Students who complete all the components of each course receive a completion card. When all fourteen modules have been completed, students receive a certificate of completion, a symbol of commitment to spiritual awakening.

This program is offered in FPMT centers around the world, as a home study program and now as an interactive online program as well.

Each module of both the home study and online program contains audio recordings of teachings and meditations given by qualified Western teachers, course materials and transcripts, online discussion forum overseen by senior FPMT teachers and completion certificates. FAQ pages help the student navigate the program and provide the best of the discussion board's questions and answers. Upon completion of a module, students may have their assessment questions evaluated by senior FPMT teachers and receive personal feedback.

Both *Discovering Buddhism at Home* and *Discovering Buddhism Online* are available from the FPMT Foundation Store, www.fpmt.org/shop or by becoming a Friend of FPMT, www.fpmt.org/friends. For more information on *Discovering Buddhism* and the other educational programs and services of the FPMT, please visit us at www.fpmt.org/education.

.OTHER TEACHINGS OF LAMA YESHE AND LAMA ZOPA RINPOCHE CURRENTLY AVAILABLE

BOOKS PUBLISHED BY WISDOM PUBLICATIONS
Wisdom Energy, by Lama Yeshe and Lama Zopa Rinpoche
Introduction to Tantra, by Lama Yeshe
Transforming Problems, by Lama Zopa Rinpoche
The Door to Satisfaction, by Lama Zopa Rinpoche
Becoming Vajrasattva: The Tantric Path of Purification, by Lama Yeshe
The Bliss of Inner Fire, by Lama Yeshe
Becoming the Compassion Buddha, by Lama Yeshe
Ultimate Healing, by Lama Zopa Rinpoche
Dear Lama Zopa, by Lama Zopa Rinpoche
How to Be Happy, by Lama Zopa Rinpoche
Wholesome Fear, by Lama Zopa Rinpoche with Kathleen McDonald

About Lama Yeshe:
Reincarnation: The Boy Lama, by Vicki Mackenzie

About Lama Zopa Rinpoche:
The Lawudo Lama, by Jamyang Wangmo

You can get more information about and order the above titles at www.wisdom-pubs.org or call toll free in the USA on 1-800-272-4050.

TRANSCRIPTS, PRACTICES AND OTHER MATERIALS
See the LYWA and FPMT websites for transcripts of teachings by Lama Yeshe and Lama Zopa Rinpoche and other practices written or compiled by Lama Zopa Rinpoche.

DVDs OF LAMA YESHE
We are in the process of converting our VHS videos of Lama Yeshe's teachings to DVD. *The Three Principal Aspects of the Path, Introduction to Tantra, Offering Tsok to Heruka Vajrasattva, Anxiety in the Nuclear Age, Bringing Dharma to the West* and *Lama Yeshe at Disneyland* are currently available. More coming all the time—see our website for details.

DVDs OF LAMA ZOPA RINPOCHE
There are many available: see the Store on the FPMT website for more information.

What to do with Dharma teachings

The Buddhadharma is the true source of happiness for all sentient beings. Books like the one in your hand show you how to put the teachings into practice and integrate them into your life, whereby you get the happiness you seek. Therefore, anything containing Dharma teachings or the names of your teachers is more precious than other material objects and should be treated with respect. To avoid creating the karma of not meeting the Dharma again in future lives, please do not put books (or other holy objects) on the floor or underneath other stuff, step over or sit upon them, or use them for mundane purposes such as propping up wobbly tables. They should be kept in a clean, high place, separate from worldly writings, and wrapped in cloth when being carried around. These are but a few considerations.

Should you need to get rid of Dharma materials, they should not be thrown in the rubbish but burned in a special way. Briefly: do not incinerate such materials with other trash, but alone, and as they burn, recite the mantra OM AH HUM. As the smoke rises, visualize that it pervades all of space, carrying the essence of the Dharma to all sentient beings in the six samsaric realms, purifying their minds, alleviating their suffering, and bringing them all happiness, up to and including enlightenment. Some people might find this practice a bit unusual, but it is given according to tradition. Thank you very much.

Dedication

Through the merit created by preparing, reading, thinking about and sharing this book with others, may all teachers of the Dharma live long and healthy lives, may the Dharma spread throughout the infinite reaches of space, and may all sentient beings quickly attain enlightenment.

In whichever realm, country, area or place this book may be, may there be no war, drought, famine, disease, injury, disharmony or unhappiness, may there be only great prosperity, may everything needed be easily obtained, and may all be guided by only perfectly qualified Dharma teachers, enjoy the happiness of Dharma, have love and compassion for all sentient beings, and only benefit and never harm each other.

LAMA THUBTEN ZOPA RINPOCHE was born in Thami, Nepal, in 1945. At the age of three he was recognized as the reincarnation of the Lawudo Lama, who had lived nearby at Lawudo, within sight of Rinpoche's Thami home. Rinpoche's own description of his early years may be found in his book, *The Door to Satisfaction*. At the age of ten, Rinpoche went to Tibet and studied and meditated at Domo Geshe Rinpoche's monastery near Pagri, until the Chinese occupation of Tibet in 1959 forced him to forsake Tibet for the safety of Bhutan. Rinpoche then went to the Tibetan refugee camp at Buxa Duar, West Bengal, India, where he met Lama Yeshe, who became his closest teacher. The Lamas went to Nepal in 1967, and over the next few years built Kopan and Lawudo Monasteries. In 1971 Lama Zopa Rinpoche gave the first of his famous annual lam-rim retreat courses, which continue at Kopan to this day. In 1974, with Lama Yeshe, Rinpoche began traveling the world to teach and establish centers of Dharma. When Lama Yeshe passed away in 1984, Rinpoche took over as spiritual head of the FPMT, which has continued to flourish under his peerless leadership. More details of Rinpoche's life and work may be found in *The Lawudo Lama* and on the LYWA and FPMT websites. In addition to many LYWA and FPMT books, Rinpoche's other published teachings include *Wisdom Energy* (with Lama Yeshe), *Transforming Problems, Ultimate Healing, Dear Lama Zopa, How to Be Happy* and many transcripts and practice booklets.

DR. NICHOLAS RIBUSH, MB, BS, is a graduate of Melbourne University Medical School (1964) who first encountered Buddhism at Kopan Monastery, Nepal, in 1972. Since then he has been a student of Lama Yeshe and Lama Zopa Rinpoche and a full time worker for their international organization, the Foundation for the Preservation of the Mahayana Tradition (FPMT). He was a monk from 1974 to 1986. He established FPMT archiving and publishing activities at Kopan in 1973 and with Lama Yeshe founded Wisdom Publications in 1975. Between 1981 and 1996 he served variously as Wisdom's director, editorial director and director of development. Over the years he has edited and published many teachings by His Holiness the Dalai Lama, Lama Yeshe, Lama Zopa Rinpoche and many other teachers and established and/or directed several other FPMT activities, including the International Mahayana Institute, Tushita Mahayana Meditation Centre, the Enlightened Experience Celebration, Mahayana Publications, and now Kurukulla Center for Tibetan Buddhist Studies and the LAMA YESHE WISDOM ARCHIVE. He was a member of the FPMT board of directors from its inception in 1983 until 2002.